Anointed to Lead: The Baptismal Call of the Parish Staff is an excellent resource to nurture the spiritual and ministerial development of the staff. Fr. Stephen Wilbricht addresses the topics of parish leadership and Christian discipleship as coming from the baptismal call to holiness.

—Valerie Lee-Jeter
Music director at St. Vincent de Paul Parish,
Philadelphia

Stephen Wilbricht's *Anointed to Lead* inspires and challenges parish staff as they "animate the priestly service of parishioners." Interspersed with Wilbricht's liturgical, historical, and scriptural foundation for baptismal ecclesiology are anecdotes from a pastor, music minister, religi̶̶̶̶̶-̶
tor, and volunteer coordinator. The pr̶̶̶̶̶̶̶̶̶̶̶̶̶̶̶̶̶̶̶̶̶̶̶̶̶̶̶̶̶̶
importance of shifting pastoral think̶̶̶̶̶̶̶̶̶̶̶̶̶̶̶̶̶̶̶̶̶̶
journeying community, making God̶̶̶̶̶̶̶̶̶̶̶̶̶̶̶̶̶̶̶̶̶̶̶̶

—Mary Pa̶̶̶̶
Pastora̶̶̶̶
Presenta̶̶̶̶ ...on, Lee's Summit, MO

Anointed to Lead rejuvenates the pastoral spirit and helps fill in the gaps toward discovering our baptismal call, whether in a parish, at a diocesan level, at a non-profit organization, or simply applying it to our own personal journey.

—Yolanda Madrid
Assistant to the vice chancellor and director
of apostolic and ethnic affairs
for the Diocese of San Bernardino

In *Anointed to Lead,* Fr. Stephen Wilbricht truly presents a model for living in the parish as a royal priesthood, a holy nation, a people set apart. This model is desperately needed in a time when the Church must be a true body of common unity in Christ.

—Father Ajani K. Gibson
St. Peter Claver Catholic Church,
New Orleans

ANOINTED TO LEAD

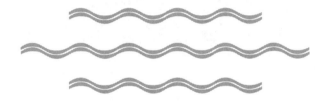

ANOINTED to Lead

The Baptismal Call of the Parish Staff

STEPHEN S. WILBRICHT, csc

WITH CONTRIBUTIONS FROM
CRISTINA CASTILLO
MICHAEL CONRADY
CAROLINE OKELLO
PATRICK A. SMITH

LTP
LITURGY
TRAINING
PUBLICATIONS

Nihil Obstat
Deacon Daniel G. Welter, JD
Chancellor
Archdiocese of Chicago
June 14, 2022

Imprimatur
Most Rev. Robert G. Casey
Vicar General
Archdiocese of Chicago
June 14, 2022

ANOINTED TO LEAD: THE BAPTISMAL CALL OF THE PARISH STAFF © 2022 Archdiocese of Chicago: Liturgy Training Publications, 3949 South Racine Avenue, Chicago, IL 60609; 800-933-1800; fax: 800-933-7094; email: orders@ltp.org; website: www.LTP.org. All rights reserved.

This book was edited by Mary G. Fox. Víctor R. Pérez was the production editor, Anna Manhart was the designer, and Juan Alberto Castillo was the production artist.

Cover and interior art by James B. Janknegt.

26 25 24 23 22   1 2 3 4 5

Printed in the United States of America

Library of Congress Control Number: 2022941582

ISBN: 978-1-61671-684-4

ATL

CONTENTS

✤

INTRODUCTION

❖

Father Patrick A. Smith poses this question to parents when he meets with them prior to their baby's baptism: "What is the date of your baptism?" The pastor of St. Augustine Church in Washington, DC, wants to ascertain whether these parents know who they are. Do they know that they are God's adopted sons and daughters? Have they reflected on that? Have they celebrated it? Do they know the duties and responsibilities that come with baptism?

Living as adopted sons and daughters means being committed to the common good, working for oneness in creation, and laboring for those who struggle to survive. Only when people know who they are can they respond to God's love in these ways. Only if they know who they are would they live as disciples of Christ. After all, Father Patrick asks, "How could 'the eyes of all believers' be open to and respond to 'the realities of suffering and injustice that exist on our planet' if they can't see the love the Father has bestowed on them; if they don't remember who they are?"

From pastors to office staff, parish administrators lead the faithful to exercise their call to discipleship and mission. The leadership of the parish animates the priestly service of all the members of the Body of Christ to go forth to minister in the world. Through the leadership of pastors, directors of religious education, liturgists, and coordinators of ministry, parishioners come to know who they are as disciples of Christ.

This book seeks to inspire Christian leadership through baptism. Chapter 1 presents baptism as the sacrament of discipleship, the primary way in which people respond to the call to follow Christ. Chapter 2 examines parish administration and how a parish might look different if leadership flowed from the discernment of charisms. In other words, how might we prayerfully call forth men and women to use their gifts for the building up of Christ's Body? Chapter 3 proposes how baptism might be a ticket for renewal and transformation of parish life, offering biblical images that demonstrate that all leadership is servant oriented. Part 2 of the book provides seven traditional descriptions of baptism that are the source for reflection and prayer. In this context, a theological reflection paves the way for further pastoral appropriation on the part of pastors and other parish leaders. On a practical level, four pastoral leaders provide reflections from their ministry in religious education, music, coordination of volunteers, or in the pastorate. These reflections offer examples of how the pastoral minister responds to an aspect of baptism in the parish and in their lives. Questions that follow the reflections will prompt discussion during a parish staff meeting on how the parish lives out these aspects of baptism. A simple prayer service concludes each chapter. May this short consideration of our common baptism help renew in us the spirit of baptismal discipleship, for from the greatest to the least, all are called not "to be served but to serve."[1]

CONTRIBUTORS

Cristina Castillo is a doctoral student at Barry University, Miami, pursuing a degree in practical theology focusing on Latino theology and ministry. Cristina holds an MA in pastoral theology from Loyola Marymount University and a BA in political science and history from Mount St. Mary's University—both in Los Angeles. She is the former regional coordinator for the Parish Ministry Formation Program for the Diocese of San Bernardino. In that capacity, Cristina oversaw and directed the basic theology program in the region. For four years, she served as director of religious education for a parish in the Archdiocese of Los Angeles.

---

1. Matthew 20:28.

Michael Conrady, DMIN, is a pastoral musician and educator. He serves as the organist and choirmaster at St. Thomas Aquinas Catholic Church in Dallas, Texas, where he oversees an active parish music program. He holds degrees from Baylor University (BBA) and Southern Methodist University (MM, MSM, MTS, and DMIN). His doctoral thesis concentrated on medieval Communion antiphons and the composition of new music for use in the Roman Catholic liturgy. In 2019, Dr. Conrady joined the faculty at the University of North Texas, where he teaches undergraduate and graduate courses in sacred music. In addition to parish ministry and teaching, he serves on a number of organizations dedicated to liturgy and pastoral music.

Caroline Okello is the volunteer coordinator at St. James Cathedral, Seattle, Washington. She was born in Homa Bay, Kenya, migrated to the United States in 2009, and became a US citizen in 2016. Her bachelor's degree in business administration is from the University of Nairobi, Kenya. In Kenya and Rwanda, she worked for international and nonprofit organizations, including the International Committee of the Red Cross and International Federation of the Red Cross and Red Crescent Societies. Among her volunteer work, she has spearheaded the sewing of reusable hygiene kits for girls in Africa. The kits have gone to Kenya, Tanzania, Uganda, Malawi, and Burkina Faso.

Father Patrick A. Smith is the pastor of St. Augustine Church, Washington, DC, the oldest Black church in the nation's capital. A priest for over thirty years, he is sought out as a speaker, preacher, revivalist, and retreat director for youth and adults. His BA in sacred theology and his license in sacred theology are from the North American College in Rome. His thesis at the Pontifical University of St. Thomas Aquinas in Rome was on a study of Martin Luther King Jr.

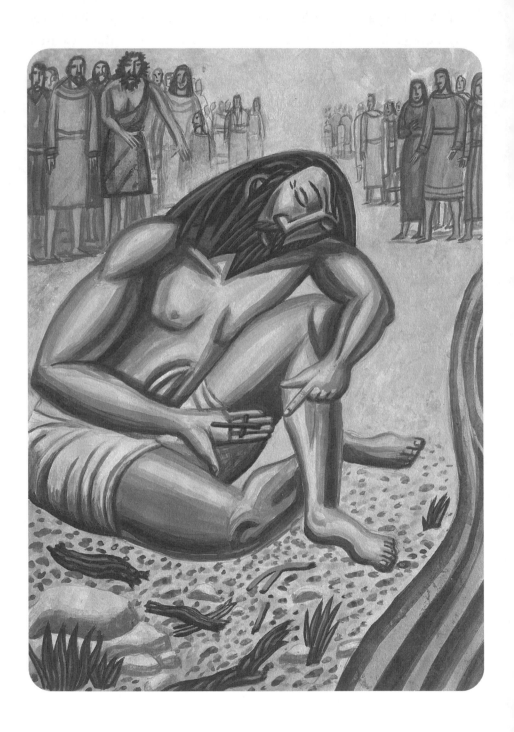

PART 1

THE COMMUNAL NATURE OF BAPTISM

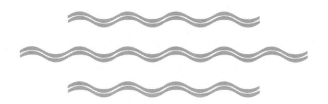

CHAPTER 1

Baptism as the Foundation of the Church

Go, therefore, and make disciples of all nations, baptizing them in the name of the Father, and of the Son, and of the holy Spirit, teaching them to observe all that I have commanded you. And behold, I am with you always, until the end of the age.

—Matthew 28:19–20

Since its very foundation, the Christian community has understood that the perpetuation of Christ's ministry involves the ritual of baptism.[1] Baptism is the primary way in which men and women respond to the call to follow Jesus. The call of Peter, Andrew, James, and John, in which these men abandon Zebedee in the boat and follow Jesus (Matthew 4:18–22), is not baptism per se. Nevertheless, the invitation to completely abandon a way of life to become immersed in the adventure that Jesus was about to begin with his ministry is baptismal indeed. In fact, the Greek verb *bautizein* means "to immerse," and surely that is what the first four disciples did as they turned their backs on the shores of Galilee, left their well-worn nets, and plunged themselves into

---

1. Much of the material in this chapter is adapted from the chapter "What Is Baptismal Ecclesiology?" in my book *Baptismal Ecclesiology* and the Order of Christian Funerals (Chicago: Liturgy Training Publications, 2019).

the mystery of journeying with Jesus as he went about proclaiming God's kingdom.

First and foremost, Christian baptism entails discipleship. Jesus calls people to challenging work. Those who enter the font, whether they be mature adults or newborn infants, embark upon a completely new way of life that is, simply put, life with Christ. This life gives the newly baptized an entirely new set of relationships—namely, the bonds of unity that are meant to be forged among all the baptized and that are meant to heal the brokenness of the world. This means that just as Jesus walked this earth announcing a kingdom that would unite all creation in God's love, so too does baptism perpetuate this ministry in the contemporary world. Those who are baptized in Christ are called to proclaim the good news with their lives and to anticipate the coming of the kingdom through the attitude of hope. Baptism is all about mission.

Yet quite early within the spectrum of Christian history, the sacrament of baptism lost its connection to discipleship. The explanation for this loss is quite simple. As Christianity grew in numbers and spread beyond the Mediterranean world, the majority of candidates to be baptized were infants. Additionally, the development of the doctrine of original sin, largely attrib-

Baptism is a daily event in which individuals die to themselves to live in Christ, awakening the world to the truth of salvation.

uted to the theology of St. Augustine (354–430), would shift the dominant meaning of baptism from discipleship to the freedom from the stain of sin caused by Adam and Eve. Baptism was now all about the salvation of one's soul. Consequently, baptism quickly came to be interpreted as a once-in-a-lifetime moment in which a person is born as a new creation, worthy of God's love and care. What is lost is the notion that baptism is a daily event in which individuals die to themselves to live in Christ, awakening the world to the truth of salvation. Like so much of life today, baptism has become privatized, individualized, and commodified (something purchased only to be quickly forgotten).

Since the Second Vatican Council much has been done to restore the understanding of baptism as the primary sacrament for discipleship. The underlying question to be resolved is this: Is baptism primarily a sacrament concerning the individual soul and its destiny to be with God in heaven? Or is baptism primarily a sacrament that concerns the whole Church on its pilgrim journey toward salvation with God? Both answers can be deemed to be correct, but the documents of the Second Vatican Council seem to emphasize corporate discipleship as the most fulfilling way to understand baptism. In fact, the opening words of *Lumen gentium* (LG), the council's *Dogmatic Constitution on the Church*, far from envisioning the Church as a collection of redeemed individuals, refers to the Church as a "sacrament" of unity among disciples:

> Since the church, in Christ, is a sacrament—a sign and instrument, that is, of communion with God and of the unity of the entire human race—it here proposes, for the benefit of the faithful and of the entire world, to describe more clearly, and in the tradition laid down by earlier council, its own nature and universal mission.[2]

As both "sign and instrument," the Church strives to enact communion as both a marker of her self-identity as well as a means of prophesying to the entire world. The sacrament of baptism introduces new members into the Body of Christ, and the celebration of the Eucharist puts those relationships back together again, arranging them anew, each time the community assembles around the Lord's table.

Unity, or communion, is precisely the sacramental nature of the Church, or what the Church is called to make visibly present to the world. In his extensive preaching, the apostle Paul used the "Body of Christ" as a primary image of the Church. Just as the parts of the human body are both numerous and diverse, so too are the many members

---

2. *Lumen gentium* (LG), 1.

of the Body of Christ (1 Corinthians 12:12). *Lumen gentium* elaborates on the Church as a unified body:

> In this body the life of Christ is communicated to those who believe and who, through the sacraments, are united in a hidden and real way to Christ in his passion and glorification. Through Baptism we are formed in the likeness of Christ: "For in one Spirit we were all baptized into one body" (1 Corinthians 12:13). In this sacred rite our union with Christ's death and resurrection is symbolized and effected. "For we were buried with him by Baptism into death"; and if "we have been united with him in likeness of his death, we shall be so in the likeness of his resurrection also" (Romans 6:45).[3]

As this paragraph continues, it notes the diversity of members and gifts within the body. Unity is not achieved through uniformity or through every part functioning the same way; rather, unity is based upon an appreciation of the contribution of each member:

> A diversity of members and functions is engaged in the building up of Christ's body, too. There is only one Spirit who, out of his own richness and the needs of the ministries, gives his various gifts for the welfare of the church (see 1 Corinthians 12:1–11). . . . The same Spirit who of himself is the principle of unity in the body, by his own power and by the interior cohesion of the members produces and stimulates love among the faithful. From this it follows that if one member suffers in any way, all the members suffer, and if one member is honored, all the members together rejoice (see 1 Corinthians 12:26).[4]

Without naming it as such, the Fathers of the Second Vatican Council, by examining the Church through the lens of baptism and the relationship of the faithful through the bonds forged in Christ, developed a "baptismal ecclesiology." As Paul instructs the infant Church at Galatia,

---

3. LG, 7.
4. LG, 7.

due to a common baptism, "there is neither Jew nor Greek, there is neither slave nor free person, there is not male and female; for you are all one in Christ Jesus" (Galatians 3:28). Quite simply, baptismal ecclesiology underscores the fundamental oneness of the Body of Christ; how the Church organizes her institutional structures and how she enacts ministry in the world are to bear witness to this principle of unity. As ecclesiologist Michael Fahey writes: "The emphasis is not on the role of Christians taken as individuals but rather as members of the body of Christ. The faithful find their dignity rooted in the gift of baptism through which even as lay persons they share in the priestly and prophetic office of Christ."[5]

There are objections to this theology that must be acknowledged at the outset. First is the simple recognition that the division among the Christian churches is a scandal that diminishes the truth that there exists a divine unity in the Body of Christ. Again, quoting Fahey: "The most obvious fact about the Christian church today is that it is divided. Not only are the churches of the East and the West existentially estranged and still living in mutual suspicion of one another after over a millennium, but the churches of the West themselves have been tragically fragmented since the sixteenth century."[6] There is no doubt that Christians are divided over such topics as the ordering of ministry, apostolic succession, papal primacy, women's ordination, and some moral issues. However, since the time of the Second Vatican Council, Christians have made great progress in coming to adhere to the principle that baptism establishes a unity among all members of Christ. Such agreement is beautifully expressed in the 1982 paper *Baptism, Eucharist and Ministry*, prepared by a worldwide team of Christian scholars:

---

5. Michael A. Fahey, "Church," in *Systematic Theology: Roman Catholic Perspectives*, vol. 2, ed. Francis Schüssler Fiorenza and John Galvin (Minneapolis, MN: Fortress Press, 1991), 44.
6. Fahey, "Church," 6.

Administered in obedience to our Lord, baptism is a sign and seal of our common discipleship. Through baptism, Christians are brought into union with Christ, with each other and with the Church of every time and place. Our common baptism, which unites us to Christ in faith, is thus a basic bond of unity. We are one people and are called to confess and serve one Lord in each place and in all the world. The union with Christ which we share through baptism has important implications for Christian unity. "There is . . . one baptism, one God and Father of us all . . . " (Ephesians 4:4–6). When baptismal unity is recognized in one holy, catholic, apostolic Church, a genuine Christian witness can be made to the healing and reconciling love of God. Therefore, our one baptism in Christ constitutes a call to the churches to overcome their divisions and visibly manifest their fellowship.[7]

While it may be the case that division prevails on the surface of relationships within different types of Christian assemblies, the oneness that is Christ is the invisible bond that necessarily unites all disciples. Fortunately, the work of restoring unity within Christianity has been less about mandating that all Christians return to Roman Catholicism than about helping Christians to recognize and honor a diversity of ways for following Christ, for worshiping God, and therefore, for forming one Christian Church. In the words of Walter Kasper, "Church and baptism belong together from the very beginning. . . . Hence the ecumenical movement from the start has sought to make our common baptism the point of departure and the basis for ecumenical efforts."[8]

A second critique of the Pauline theology regarding the unity of the Body of Christ that flows from the sacrament of baptism fears that such an approach tries to erase personal identity. In other words, while

---

7. *Baptism, Eucharist and Ministry*, Faith and Order Paper, 111 (Geneva: Would Council of Churches, 1982), paragraph 6, page 2.

8. Walter Kasper, "Ecclesiological and Ecumenical Implications of Baptism," *The Ecumenical Review* 52 (2000): 526.

oneness in Christ may at first seem to embrace diversity in its entirety, some believe that it creates a sense of neutrality that does not truly honor and celebrate diverse gifts and traits. Thus, while a liturgical assembly may be composed of different colors, sexes, economic classes, ages, and lifestyles—together forming "one body in Christ"—some would say that people have been merely lumped together without any acknowledgment of the beauty of difference. For example, Bryan Cones writes: "Thus, while a diverse assembly is the presumed goal and fullest liturgical symbol, it is an assembly in which all that difference is . . . 'lumped' together into a harmonious unity, rather than 'split' in ways to make visible the diversity present—and to interrogate the relationships among those differences."[9] Thus, it is important to recognize that baptismal ecclesiology based on the Pauline image of the unity of Christ's Body must not be about erasing diversity, but instead must be about discerning the gifts that each one brings to the Church.

Thus, acknowledging the paramount need to heal divisions among Christians as well as resisting the temptation to equate the baptismal font with a kind of melting pot that makes all Christians the same, baptismal ecclesiology has some important ramifications regarding leadership in the Church. Such is primarily the focus of this book. If baptism is understood primarily in terms of discipleship, then each member of Christ's Body has a role to play in enacting the Church's mission in every age. Let us examine several aspects of baptism that naturally point to shared leadership in the Church.

As has been established, baptism is about the community, not solely about the individual. When a member is grafted onto the Body of Christ through the celebration of baptism, the Body necessarily changes, relationships are established and renewed, growth takes place. This means that baptism can never be a private affair; it always involves the

---

9. Bryan Cones, "'How Beautiful the Feet': Discerning the Assembly's Path on Holy Thursday," in *Liturgy with a Difference: Beyond Inclusion in the Christian Assembly*, ed. Stephen Burns and Bryan Cones (London: SCM Press, 2019), 6.

Christian community. As a result, movement is made away from an individualistic approach to anything having to do with faith, and hopefully, in anything having to do with daily life. Baptism is meant to strip away any sort of self-sufficient individualism. In 1963, C. Kilmer Myers, a theologian of the Episcopal Church, writes of the corporate nature of baptism:

> When, by God's action, we are brought into the Church, we, with all Christians, are indeed *in*. We are inside her life; her vitality passes into us. Our life is merged with her communal life. Now it is no longer "I" alone: now it is "we." Now we are a people—the people of God. We say *our* Father now, and we say *our* Lord . . . The individualist Christian is primarily concerned with the state of single souls: he says, "Jesus is my God," and he may ask, "Are you saved, Brother?" . . . When a Christian is excessively individualist, he finds it hard to grasp the Biblical doctrine of the Body of Christ. He is likely to devalue the Church's sacramental life, relegating Baptism to the area of personal salvation and looking upon the Lord's Supper as a sacramental means of personal communion with the Lord.[10]

Myers suggests, at the outset of this quote, that with baptism, we "are indeed *in*." But the question that needs to be raised in parish leadership is: Does every baptized member of the Church believe that they belong? The Church competes with so many other institutions and activities that allow people to develop a sense of belonging in areas other than their faith. For example, it is very possible that a Christian may feel a greater commitment of belonging to a gym than to the Church. Reasons that people may feel alienation from the Church need to be explored. If baptized Christians are not convinced that their presence is valued, they are certainly not going to offer themselves as leaders. The bottom line is that baptism is a great social leveler within the Church; any sense of

---

10. C. Kilmer Myers, *Baptized into the One Church* (New York: Seabury Press, 1963), 12–13.

THE COMMUNAL NATURE OF BAPTISM

individualism is wiped away by the call to communal responsibility. Every member of the Body of Christ matters.

For this reason, some Christian denominations work hard to link baptism to mission. For example, in recent decades, the Episcopal Church has created the "Baptismal Covenant" to express commitment to the corporate body of the Church.[11] The Baptismal Covenant is a set of five questions used at the celebration of baptism after the profession of the Apostles' Creed. The questions are as follows:

Celebrant: Will you continue in the apostles' teaching and fellowship, in the breaking of bread, and in the prayers?

People: I will, with God's help.

Celebrant: Will you persevere in resisting evil, and, whenever you fall into sin, repent and return to the Lord?

People: I will, with God's help.

Celebrant: Will you proclaim by word and example the Good News of God in Christ?

People: I will, with God's help.

Celebrant: Will you seek and serve Christ in all persons, loving your neighbor as yourself?

People: I will, with God's help.

Celebrant: Will you strive for justice and peace among all people, and respect the dignity of every human being?

People: I will, with God's help.[12]

---

11. See *The Book of Common Prayer and Administration of the Sacraments and Other Rites and Ceremonies of the Church . . . according to the use of the Episcopal Church* (New York: Seabury Press, 1979), 304–305.

12. I am grateful to Susan Marie Smith, who informed me that the Episcopal Church is considering a sixth question: Will you cherish the wondrous works of God and protect the beauty and integrity of all creation?

The structure of the baptismal covenant is at the same time innovative and traditional: profession of the Triune God is followed immediately by a statement of commitment to a particular way of life. Beyond the commitment to communal worship and the pursuit of personal holiness, the emphasis of the baptismal covenant is on discipleship—that is, serving Christ in all persons.

Returning to the thought of C. Kilmer Myers, whose writing predates the appearance of the baptismal covenant, baptism must necessarily be understood as the sacrament of ministry. He writes:

> By being baptized into the indivisible Body of Christ, every Christian is called to participate in the one Church's united ministry to the one world. . . . Though we have different functions and ministries, Holy Baptism is the great leveler among us. Whether we are clergymen or laymen, child or adult, by our Baptism we are drawn into the ministry of Christ. And that ministry is in the world. . . . Baptism initiates us into the holy society of servants. The ministry to which our Baptism commits us is outside the Church in the one world for which Christ died.[13]

It is true that the sacrament of holy orders, in the Roman Catholic Church, is meant to make Christ's ministry tangible and accessible to the Church. However, what is being argued here, and which does not conflict with Catholic theology, is that baptism initiates all Christians into a life of discipleship and ministry. The sacrament of holy orders serves to objectify this life for some who have been chosen by the Church. This way of thinking about the priesthood of the baptized is very much in keeping with how *Lumen gentium* describes the apostolate of the laity:

> The apostolate of the laity is a sharing in the church's saving mission. Through Baptism and Confirmation all are appointed to this apostolate by the Lord himself. . . . The laity, however, are given this

---

13. Myers, *Baptized into the One Church*, 18–20.

special vocation: to make the church present and fruitful in those places and circumstances where it is only through them that it can become the salt of the earth. Thus, all lay people, through the gifts which they have received, are at once the witnesses and the living instruments of the mission of the church itself "according to the measure of Christ's gift" (Ephesians 4:7).[14]

The question for many supporters of baptismal ecclesiology is that, because baptism is a social leveler, and because all members of the Body of Christ are considered ministers, should not this call into question the need for holy orders? An affirmative answer to this question has led the Episcopal Church to a wide-sweeping endorsement of women's ordination. As Louis Weil states: "If discernment concerning suitability for holy orders is grounded in a baptismal ecclesiology, then the fundamental issue is not a person's gender or sexual orientation, but rather the evidence of the charisms that the church needs in its ordained leaders."[15]

Although the Anglican community has focused much attention on reform based on the belief that "all Christians are empowered for ministry on the basis of their baptism alone,"[16] Roman Catholic theologians are not silent regarding the link between baptism and leadership within the community. An example of this may be found in the writing of the leader of the pre–Vatican II liturgical movement in the United States, Virgil Michel, osb, who believed that learning the socialization accomplished by liturgical prayer would necessarily lead to the rejuvenation of society as a whole. He writes:

---

14. LG, 33.

15. Louis Weil, "Baptismal Ecclesiology: Uncovering a Paradigm," in *Equipping the Saints: Ordination in Anglicanism Today*, ed. Ronald L. Dowling and David R. Holeton (Dublin: Columba Press, 2006), 26.

16. Daniel E. Joslyn-Siemiatkoski and Ruth A. Meyers, "The Baptismal Ecclesiology of *Holy Women, Holy Men*: Developments in the Theology of Sainthood in the Episcopal Church," *Anglican Theological Review* 94:1 (2012): 35.

There is only one answer I know of to the problem of the balanced harmony between the individual and the social: *The Mystical Body of Christ*. There the individual returns his full responsibility, the fullest possibility of greater realization of his dignity as a member of Christ, yet he is ever a member in the fellowship of Christ, knit closely with his fellow members into a compact body by the indwelling of the Spirit of Christ: *There* is the pattern of all social life lived by individuals.[17]

For Michel, participation in the liturgy is an experience of membership within the Body of Christ, whereby each participant enacts responsibility for others. In this setting, one ought to learn how to truly pray communally and not simply privately. "Far from depreciating or suppressing the values of individuality and personality," writes Michel, "the Mystical Body of Christ gives these their best possible realization. The responsibility that each member has, not only for his own self, but also for the good of the whole Body, is the highest personal responsibility that the individual can be privileged to share."[18] Although a social leveler, baptism into the Body of Christ is not to be equated with a political democracy comprised of equal individuals: instead it is about the communion of interpersonal relationships.[19] Have leaders worked to organize the parish through expression of personal charisms and responsibility?

The Mystical Body of Christ theology popularized in the United States as well as Europe in the early part of the twentieth century continued to be developed in and through the work of the Second Vatican Council. For example, the *Constitution on the Sacred Liturgy* (*Sacrosanctum Concilium*), states: "The liturgy is considered as an exercise of the priestly office of Jesus Christ. In the liturgy, by means of signs perceptible to the senses, human sanctification is signified and brought

---

17. Virgil Michel, "Natural and Supernatural Society," *Orate Fratres* 10 (1936): 244–245.

18. Michel, "Natural and Supernatural Society," 434–435.

19. See Michael G. Lawler and Thomas Shanahan, "The Church Is a Graced Communion," *Worship* 67 (1993): 496.

about in ways proper to each of these signs; in the liturgy the whole public worship is performed by the Mystical Body of Jesus Christ, that is, by the Head and his members."[20] Jesus Christ is the true priest who ministers in his Church; members of his Body are called upon to make his ministry tangibly present.

The way to embody this presence is through striving for communion at every level within the Church. Thus, baptismal ecclesiology is intrinsically connected to an "ecclesiology of communion."[21] "Communion ecclesiology," based on the oneness of the Body of Christ, calls for leadership that animates the priestly service of all the members of the Church. Pope John Paul II writes in his apostolic exhortation *Pastores dabo vobis* that the role of the ordained priesthood is to "promote the baptismal priesthood of the entire people of God, leading it to its full realization."[22] The key here is to truly understand the importance and the responsibility of the priesthood of all the baptized. As Paul Philibert contends:

> The fundamental consecration of every Christian, ordained or not, is baptism—the deepest ontological change that a person can experience. Baptism is the change from being ordered to death to being ordered to life eternal, the change from being linked to a destiny that ends in futility (cf. 1 Peter 1:18) to being integrated into the Body of Christ the Lord. Every other dignity and service in the Church arises out of this fundamental consecration.[23]

Again, the entire mission of the Church can be boiled down to the overturning of individualism and selfishness by the pursuit of communion. The Church is organized so as to embody communion, which necessarily is meant to be a sign and instrument of renewed relationships inside and outside of the Church. Any form of leadership within the

---

20. *Sacrosanctum Concilium* (SC), 7.

21. See Paul J. Philibert, "Reclaiming the Vision of an Apostolic Church," *Worship* 83 (2009): 484–485.

22. John Paul II, *Pastores dabo vobis*, 17.

23. Philibert, "Reclaiming the Vision of an Apostolic Church," 494–495.

Church must be based on the pursuit and enactment of communion. Richard Gaillardetz writes:

> [W]hen ministry is considered within the context of this relational ontology the minister is seen fundamentally as a servant of communion. This image of ministry is multi-dimensional but gives primacy to the affirmation and nurturance of authentic human relationships which are inclusive, mutual, reciprocal and generative, and the condemnation of relationships of manipulation, domination and subordination as sinful perversions of the call to human communion. It is a vision capable of realization in every concrete ministry, ordained and nonordained, professional and occasional. . . . Finally, the life of communion has its origins in the deepest yearnings of the human spirit for true communion with another and, ultimately, true communion with God. Therefore, the minister, as servant of communion, is at the same time, servant of the Church, servant of God and servant of humankind.[24]

At stake here is a call to recognize baptism as the sacrament of discipleship. Baptism is so much more than the cleansing of original sin and the adoption by God of new members into his household. Also at stake is the need for parish leaders to recognize the importance of our common baptism. All are meant to lead through their baptism. Parish leadership is at its best when everything it does revolves around the desire to assist the communion of the faithful; everything it does ought to flow from the desire to be one. Kathleen Cahalan depicts a life of Christian discipleship as follows:

Parish leadership is at its best when everything it does revolves around the desire to assist the communion of the faithful; everything it does ought to flow from the desire to be one.

---

24. Richard R. Gaillardetz, "In Service of Communion: A Trinitarian Foundation for Christian Ministry," *Worship* 67 (1993): 432–433.

Discipleship is not an achievement. It is an identity, a commitment, a way of life, and a response to a call. . . . To be a disciple means to be a follower of Christ, committed to learning his ways, to be a worshiper, joining Christ and the community in praise of God's wonders; to be a forgiver by practicing reconciliation, healing and peacemaking; to be a neighbor by living mindfully of others' needs and reaching out to them with compassion; to be a prophet willing to tell the truth about the injustices that harm neighbors; and to be stewards of the creation, the community, and the mysteries of faith.[25]

Baptism is the sacrament that serves as the foundation of the Church and the entirety of its ministerial life. Thus, Susan Wood rightfully calls baptism the "primary sacrament of ministry." She writes:

Baptism initiates a person as a member of the community, and ministry arises from the community. Through baptism we participate in the three-fold office of Christ as priest, prophet, and king. Thus, all the baptized share in the priesthood of Christ in diverse ways within the royal priesthood of the baptized. Baptism is the primary sacrament of ministry. Ordained ministry does not have a different source, but finds its source in baptism, as does lay ministry. All ordained ministry, as all discipleship, proceeds from baptism. Priests "are disciples of the Lord along with all the faithful" and "in common with all who have been reborn in the font of Baptism, are brothers among brothers and sisters as members of the same body of Christ which all are commanded to build." The priesthood of the sacrament of orders serves the priesthood of the people of God.[26]

---

25. Kathleen A. Cahalan, "Toward a Fundamental Theology of Ministry," *Worship* 80 (2006): 115.

26. Susan K. Wood, "Conclusion: Convergence Points toward a Theology of Ordered Ministries," in *Ordering the Baptismal Priesthood: Theologies of Lay and Ordained Ministry*, ed. Susan K. Wood (Collegeville, MN: Liturgical Press, 2003), 257. The quoted material is from paragraph 1 of the Second Vatican Council's *Decree on the Ministry and Life of Priests* (*Presbyterorum ordinis* [PO]).

For all the baptized to fulfill their role as priests, they must recognize that they are doing so for a priestly people, not on their own behalf. The forces of individualism rage in every aspect of life in the twenty-first century, and even baptism is subject to turning solely to the individual. Thus, we have much work to do to renew the understanding that baptism is for the Church and the Church is for the world.

❖ Discussion Questions ❖

1. Reflect on both your vocational and routine choices and decisions. How has your baptism informed them?

2. Just before ascending to heaven, Christ left his disciples with the words, "Go, therefore, and make disciples of all nations, baptizing them in the name of the Father, and of the Son, and of the holy Spirit, teaching them to observe all that I have commanded." When did you first realize that baptism is about the mission of the Church?

3. Do certain members of the staff excel at animating the priestly service of parishioners? Explore ways for that person to help other members of the staff develop that part of their ministry.

4. Brainstorm ways that the staff could work together to animate parishioners' priestly service.

5. How does a consideration of the communal nature of baptism broaden your understanding of the sacrament?

CHAPTER 2

Baptism as the Heart of Parish Administration

Having established the sacrament of baptism as the sacrament of Christian discipleship, and thus the foundation of the Church and its mission to spread the good news of the kingdom far and wide, we now turn to communities of faith. All Christians are called individually by name to serve Christ with their gifts and talents. What we call the "Church" is thereby formed in the uniting of members into Christ's Body. Liturgically speaking, communion is something we become, not something we receive.

For many centuries, especially since the Protestant Reformation in the sixteenth century, there have been diverse ways of establishing Christian communities. The Roman Catholic Church, relying heavily on the sacraments and visible manifestations of unity (that is, apostolic succession) is organized hierarchically. Chapter 3 of *Lumen gentium*, "The Church Is Hierarchical," begins:

> In order to ensure that the people of God would have pastors and would enjoy continual growth, Christ the Lord set up in his church a variety of offices whose aim is the good of the whole body. Ministers, invested with a sacred power, are at the service of their brothers and sisters, so that all who belong to the people of God and therefore

enjoy true christian dignity may attain to salvation through their free, combined and well-ordered efforts in pursuit of a common goal.[1]

Thus, the primary purpose for the hierarchy of the Catholic Church is twofold: for the provision of pastors and for the calling forth of new disciples in every age. All Christian communities certainly share the concern of guaranteeing that their people will be shepherded by pastors of good will and that women and men will hear the good news and be converted to Christ. However, many Christian communities do not share the Roman Catholic need for a governance rooted in apostolic succession and marked by the celebration of institutionalized sacraments. Christians around the world are not in agreement as to what leadership should look like.

Perhaps part of the reason for this struggle is that there is no universal agreement as to what the local church ought to look like. For instance, a massive nondenominational Christian assembly in the suburbs of a major city may draw people from miles and miles away who gather almost like an audience to listen to dramatic preaching and to be inspired by contemporary music. On the other hand, a Mennonite community might depend upon a much smaller, close-knit set of relationships that center around Bible study, neighborly charity, and a way of life that is marked by austerity. In both cases, church leadership will generally craft programs and ministerial opportunities designed to bring people together. However, the communities that they are interested in building up will appear very different.

With such divergence in approaches to Christian community, we need to ask the basic question: What is a Catholic parish today? Canon law defines a parish both territorially and according to its administration. First, canon 518 states: "As a general rule a parish is to be territorial,

---

1. LG, 18.

that is, one that includes all the Christian faithful of a certain territory."[2] Second, canon 519 follows up with the definition of a "pastor":

The pastor (*parochus*) is the proper pastor (*pastor*) of the parish entrusted to him, exercising the pastoral care of the community committed to him under the authority of the diocesan bishop in whose ministry of Christ he has been called to share, so that for that same community he carries out the functions of teaching, sanctifying, and governing, also with the cooperation of other presbyters or deacons with the assistance of lay members of the Christian faithful, according to the norms of law.[3]

It is important to notice that while canon law gives very little explanation as to what constitutes a parish, other than its territorial nature, it is quite specific about the role of the pastor. A bishop is to work to ensure that a newly appointed pastor is a person of "competence."[4] Furthermore, canon 528 outlines two chief obligations of the pastor: (1) "The pastor is obliged to make provision so that the word of God is proclaimed in its entirety to those living in the parish," and (2) "The pastor is to see to it that the Most Holy Eucharist is the center of the parish assembly of the faithful." Thus, a pastor's primary identity must be rooted in the pastoral duties of preaching and celebrating the sacraments.

The first paragraph of canon 529 truly captures the many ways in which a pastor's position in the parish is that of a shepherd entrusted with the care of his flock. A pastor must embody the charism of a pastoral caregiver, a charism that is evidenced in a variety of ways:

In order to fulfill his office diligently, a pastor is to strive to know the faithful entrusted to his care. Therefore he is to visit families, sharing especially in the cares, anxieties, and griefs of the faithful,

---

2. *Code of Canon Law Latin-English Edition* (Washington, DC: Canon Law Society of America, 1983), canon 518.

3. Canon 519.

4. See canon 524.

strengthening them in the Lord, and prudently correcting them if they are failing in certain area. With generous love he is to help the sick, particularly those close to death, by refreshing them solicitously with the sacraments and commending their souls to God; with particular diligence he is to seek out the poor, the afflicted, the lonely, those exiled from their country, and similarly those weighed down with special difficulties. He is to work so that spouses and parents are supported in fulfilling their proper duties and is to foster growth in the Christian life in the family.[5]

Every obligation in canon 529 comes down to the pastor striving to know his people. He is to make a deliberate and concerted effort to know both the joys and the struggles of the faithful. He is to seek out those who are hurting in any way, and he is to be proactive in making sure that parishioners are living up to their baptismal responsibilities.

The second paragraph of canon 529 suggests that a pastor is to possess a collaborative spirit, for the sake of realizing communion within the parish and within the larger diocese. Such collaboration demonstrates the pastor's desire to truly know the faithful:

The fruit of a pastor's hard work will be the bonds of love that have been forged within the community.

The pastor is to acknowledge and promote the proper role which the lay members of the Christian faithful have in the Church's mission by fostering their associations for religious purposes; he is to cooperate with his own bishop and with the presbyterate of the diocese in working hard so that the faithful be concerned for parochial communion and that they realize that they are members both of the diocese and of the universal Church and participate in and support efforts to promote such communion.[6]

---

5. Canon 529.

6. Canon 529.

THE COMMUNAL NATURE OF BAPTISM

Clearly, what is suggested here is that the fruit of a pastor's hard work will be the bonds of love that have been forged within the community. In chapter 2 of the Second Vatican Council's *Decree on the Ministry and Life of Priests* (*Presbyterorum ordinis* [PO]), after describing the priest's role in terms of preaching and presiding at the sacraments, the focus turns to the building up of the Christian community. This section begins: "In the name of the bishop they (priests and pastors) gather the family of God as sisters and brothers endowed with the spirit of unity and lead it in Christ through the Spirit to God the Father."[7] For this reason, priests have been given "a spiritual power" which is to be used "to build up the church." Finally, "In building up a community of Christians, priests can never be the servants of any human ideology or party. Rather, their task as heralds of the Gospel and pastors of the church is the attainment of the spiritual growth of the body of Christ."[8]

It should not come as a surprise that canon law envisions parish life as flowing from the ministry of the priest/pastor. However, this may need to be rethought in the twenty-first century, when priests are installed as pastors of more than one territorial parish. A 2019 edition of *America* reports that 20 percent of all Catholic parishes in the United States (or 3,363 out of 17,007 parishes) do not have a resident pastor.[9] If one of the primary roles of a pastor is to know his people, how is this truly possible if he does not live amongst them? It seems quite unfair to divide a priest's responsibility and expect him to

> The building up of the Body of Christ takes place through the discernment of the Spirit's work.

---

7. PO, 6.

8. PO, 6.

9. Robert David Sullivan, "Parishes without Pastors Decline, But Only Because More Churches Have Closed," *America* (June 14, 2019). https://www.americamagazine.org/faith/2019/06/14/parishes-without-pastors-decline-only-because-more-churches-have-closed.

be able to know the people of the parish with the same depth of a shepherd knowing his sheep.

Thus, the building up of the Body of Christ depends upon more than the charism of the pastor. All must take part in this work. The building up of the Body of Christ takes place through the discernment of the Spirit's work. When we discover and identify the ways in which the Spirit has moved within the Church, we grow in maturity as Christ's Body. Consider the words of St. Paul in his First Letter to the Corinthians:

> There are different kinds of spiritual gifts but the same Spirit; there are different forms of service but the same Lord; there are different workings but the same God who produces all of them in everyone. To each individual the manifestation of the Spirit is given for some benefit. To one is given through the Spirit the expression of wisdom; to another the expression of knowledge according to the same Spirit; to another faith by the same Spirit; to another gifts of healing by the one Spirit; to another mighty deeds; to another prophecy; to another discernment of spirits; to another varieties of tongues; to another interpretation of tongues. But one and the same Spirit produces all of these, distributing them individually to each person as he wishes.[10]

In Paul's description of the distribution of gifts, he makes certain that the Spirit is recognized as the giver. While human recipients are meant to work with and develop the gifts they have been given, they are better thought of as stewards of particular gifts rather than sole possessors. For this reason, it is most helpful when other members of the Body are able to call forth gifts that they witness in others.

Thus, in Mystical Body theology, or in an ecclesiology based on the oneness of the Body of Christ, discernment is a key tool. For the Body to grow and flourish, the members must discern together what gifts to best employ given particular situations and moments in history.

---

10. 1 Corinthians 12:4–11.

However, communal discernment is difficult and takes a willingness to see the Christian life as an ongoing journey or pilgrimage. Herein lies the collaborative work undertaken by the pastor and the lay staff of the parish—that is, to frame the structure and operation of the parish community in a model that discerns the giftedness of the baptized. The Second Vatican Council's *Pastoral Constitution on the Church in the Modern World* (*Gaudium et spes* [GS]) envisions the work of the Church to be always "the responsibility of reading the signs of the times and of interpreting them in the light of the Gospel."[11] This document begins with a pastoral approach to understanding the world:

> The joys and hopes, the grief and anguish of the people of our time, especially of those who are poor or afflicted, are the joys and hopes, the grief and anguish of the followers of Christ as well. Nothing that is genuinely human fails to find an echo in their hearts. For theirs is a community of people united in Christ and guided by the holy Spirit in their pilgrimage towards the Father's kingdom, bearers of a message of salvation for all of humanity.[12]

Discernment demands that the Church journey with people from every walk of life and to truly try and understand life from their perspective. Luke's story of the disciples on the road to Emmaus (Luke 24:13–35) is a perfect example of two disciples who have closed themselves off to the world due to their grief, the death of their master teacher. However, the presence of a stranger among them who opened the Scriptures to them reveals the presence of the risen Lord in their midst. The discernment that took place, transforming grief-stricken hearts to ones that

What we see in the Emmaus story is that the fruit of good discernment is the presence of the risen Lord in the midst of his Body.

---

11. *Gaudium et spes* (GS), 4.
12. GS, 1.

"burned" with new life, depended on an objective individual helping them to see reality in a truthful way. What we see in the Emmaus story is that the fruit of good discernment is the presence of the risen Lord in the midst of his Body. This, in fact, is what all sacramental celebration is about, beholding the risen Christ alive in our midst.

Let us contemplate how such communal service might serve the mission of parish administration. Assuming that all baptized Christians have gifts that are meant to be used for the building up of the Body of Christ, how might parish leadership better embrace discernment as a method for the calling forth of these gifts and for their use within the Church? In his book *Discernment: Theology and Practice, Communal and Personal*, Ladislas Orsy, sj, describes this quality of leadership as follows:

> Each community within the Church is an organized body; it is alive when there is a dynamic interplay among the members. It must have a center where one (or several) person(s) clothed with authority stand and to whom informational data flow steadily from all directions. The task of the center is to create one mind and one heart in the community, out of the multiplicity of ideas and desires, in harmony with the aspirations of the universal Church. Such organic unity among intelligent persons cannot arise if those in authority alone decide all issues and call for an unconditional and blind surrender in others. The ones who preside must respond in a spirit of service to the right and just desires of all.[13]

Perhaps the greatest contribution that Orsy's project makes for our consideration of parish leadership is his overall understanding of the manner of discipleship in the Christian way. Just as we might say that baptism is a daily event that calls upon disciples to make a daily choice to follow the Lord, Orsy is clear that communal discernment focuses

---

13. Ladislas Orsy, sj, *Discernment: Theology and Practice, Communal and Personal* (Collegeville, MN: Liturgical Press, 2020), 7.

simply on helping the community make the next best step forward in life. He writes:

> A Christian community is God's pilgrim people. He leads them by twists and turns toward the Promised Land. Their pilgrimage may include events analogous to those recounted in the Bible: the flight from Egypt, the hurried wading through the Sea of Reeds, the confused and seemingly aimless wandering in the desert, the perilous conquest of their new home against fierce resistance, and, finally, the daily work of sowing seeds, planting vineyards, threshing wheat, and treading grapes. Our modern pilgrimage, no less than the old, is a journey into the unknown among many uncertainties. It requires much patience! God has his own ways and no one can force his hand. Communal discernment is not meant to lay the future bare. Christ made no such promise to his disciples. . . . Community discernment, then, is not a means to detect the future. It has a different purpose: it helps the community to become aware of the next step and gives them the strength to take it—be it through the desert, in the battle, or in carrying out the mandate of bringing the good news to all people. [14]

Each day Christians around the world utter the Lord's Prayer. This is really the prayer of Christian pilgrimage, a prayer that marks each day as a new beginning. Not only do we ask God to sustain us with "daily bread" and to "forgive us" for our wrongdoings, but we acknowledge that God's will "be done." Our role as Christian disciples is not to know the will of God for all times but rather to cooperate with the unfolding of God's will in our daily lives. Leadership that is rooted in the prayerful discernment of God's will, especially in interpreting how best to utilize the spiritual gifts that are a part of the Body of Christ, sees the Christian life from the perspective of a daily, communal journey.

---

14. *Discernment*, 35.

For parish renewal to take place in the twenty-first century, the power and authority of our baptism must be reclaimed. The roles and responsibilities of the pastor and of those in leadership positions on the parish staff, from the administrative support staff (people such as office managers and secretaries) to professional lay ministers (directors of faith formation, pastoral associates, directors of liturgy and music, financial officers) are diverse and demanding. Each of these leaders has a different perspective on the gifts that individual members offer to the Body of Christ. Pastors must share the work of discernment with the staff; and parish leadership, in turn, must seek to discern with the entire community. Thus, the next chapter will explore how a serious commitment to attend to our baptismal calling and dignity will lead to a transformation of relationships within the parish and with the outside world, thereby producing vital images for leadership.

❖ Discussion Questions ❖

1. How can the parish staff work together to call forth the gifts of the Spirit in each other? In parishioners?

2. Have you considered your baptism as something that has power and authority? Or do you usually think of it as an event that occurred in your past?

3. How might your parish be different if parishioners understood the power of their baptism?

4. Is there training that the parish staff needs to learn how to discern and to journey with others?

5. What does it mean to see the Christian life from the perspective of a daily, communal journey?

CHAPTER 3

Baptismal Transformation of the Christian Community

I n the previous chapter, we saw that baptismal ecclesiology, or understanding the Church from the perspective of our baptism, calls for a
unity in diversity that takes seriously the gifts that each baptized
Christian offers for the building up of the Body of Christ. In turn, this
suggests that the best model for parish leadership is one that is rooted in
the discernment of gifts. Also discovered is that such a model envisions
the Christian life as an event that unfolds gradually, on a daily basis,
meaning that discernment responds more to the immediate need than
it does to future goals. This chapter looks briefly at the way in which
leadership rooted in baptism serves to transform the Church and its
commitments, concluding with images for discipleship in the twenty-
first century.

One of the chief contributions of the discernment of gifts is that it
trains those involved to listen. In the context of the parish, it is quite
common for the pastor and other leaders to determine what the people
need without listening to them. For example, a pastor struggles with the
fact that parishioners across the board are not engaged in singing during
Mass, thereby not fulfilling the duty of "full, conscious, and active
participation."[1] As a result, he decides to remove the song books from

---

1. See SC, 14.

the pews and insists that all parishioners purchase a song book for their use. He reasons that, if people buy their songbook and bring it to Mass, they will be sure to sing. The problem here is that the rather silly solution to the lack of singing has not engaged the people and has not sought to gather their perspective. Consequently, the pastor fails to know the people on a deeper level.

Again, the previous example may have been extreme (although a true scenario), but it points to the reality that listening to one another is necessary for unity in diversity in the Body of Christ. Another example, one that is far from silly and in fact very serious, is the role of women in our Church. Given that women do not have positions of leadership in the hierarchy of the Catholic Church, it is harder to hear and represent their perspective. Although Pope Francis has very recently reiterated the position that women cannot be ordained, he has made small steps in expanding the leadership role of women in the Church.[2]

If we believe that baptism into Christ destroys boundaries that make distinctions between male and female, the local parish has to be a place where the voice of women is heard and given a role in discernment equal to that of men. For far too long, some have interpreted Scripture and tradition in such a way as to suggest that the suppression of women's voices is divinely willed and necessary for the natural order of things. Moreover, placing women on the margins has allowed for the development of the belief that men "are holier and more fully symbolic of Christ and God than women are."[3] Arguing that, more than ever before, the world needs the Church to be a sign and instrument of God's desire for the unity of all creation, with the exclusion of women being a countersign to this unity, theologian Mary Doak writes:

---

2. See Elisabetta Provoledo, "Pope Formalizes Women's Roles, but Priesthood Stays Out of Reach," *The New York Times*, January 11, 2021. https://www.nytimes.com/2021/01/11/world/europe/pope-women.html.

3. Mary Doak, *A Prophetic, Public Church: Witness to Hope amid the Global Crises of the Twenty-First Century* (Collegeville, MN: Liturgical Press, 2020), 91.

The ongoing challenge for the church is to affirm the full equality of women and men on the one hand, while also making room for genuine difference, including differences that do not fit into a gender binary, on the other hand. . . . The point is not to deny sexual and gender differences but to embrace the full variety of healthy sexual embodiment as experienced across race, class, culture, ethnicity, and time. . . . A true ecclesial witness to unity-in-diversity is one that affirms gender plurality as a dimension of human embodiment in a way that reinforces rather than eclipses the fundamental Christian commitment to a common human nature and the equality of baptism.[4]

Subscribing to Paul's teaching that baptism strips away identity as male or female does not mean that women and men must approach life in the same way; rather, it means simply that their primary identity is Christ. What is called for is an honoring of the unity of diversity that continues after baptism. If we honor one another as fellow members of Christ, then our differences are equally valued. Making sure that women have an active voice in the work of discernment is fundamental if we are truly going to listen to the Body of Christ.

However, it is not only the perspective of women that needs to be heard. Parish leadership needs to work to listen to all who do not fit into the majority or mainstream of the parish community. For instance, there are many people who participate in worship infrequently, who arrive and depart silently, and who are really unknown. It is important to try to come to know their life situation. They matter to the Body of Christ. As Bryan Cones and Stephen Burns write: "In effect, even while the language of 'diversity' and 'inclusion' may sometimes be sprinkled around the churches, liturgical practices of exclusion still

> Parish leadership needs to work to listen to all who do not fit into the majority or mainstream of the parish community.

---

4. Doak, *A Prophetic, Public Church*, 111.

dominate, propelling much human difference to the shadows of the liturgical assembly rather than drawing those who bear such difference to the centre, where they arguably belong."[5] To discern the gifts of the Body of Christ, parish leaders must seek out the marginalized and those who appear different than the majority.

With this kind of work at its forefront, the Church is certain to become humbler, more accepting, more hospitable. Richard Gaillardetz has recently proposed the need for a "kenotic ecclesiology" in which the Church seeks to empty itself of any sort of divine privilege, which in turn exhibits the servant nature of the Church. He writes:

> We begin each celebration of the Eucharist with a penitential rite in which we profess our sinfulness and need for forgiveness, prayer and support; we confess our unworthiness before coming to the eucharistic table. These liturgical acts of repentance are more than an aggregation of individual confessions; they are *ecclesial* performances. Out of this penitential spirit and practice should arise an ecclesial humility that finds solidarity in the company of sinners and sees our church afresh in both its indefectible holiness and its undeniable sinfulness. A truly repentant and human church is a church that renounces moral superiority and exclusivism and encourages a spirit of hospitality toward all.[6]

Parish leadership bears the task of witnessing to such hospitality and openness for the purpose of inspiring all to follow in step. Members of the Body of Christ are called upon to scrutinize their demeanor and attitudes and to ask how they might provide a more accepting welcome of people from every walk of life. This is a matter of humble service.

As the number of Catholics participating in regular Sunday liturgy continues to decrease, with one recent poll estimating that only four out

---

5. Bryan Cones and Stephen Burns, "Introduction: The Vivid Richness of God's Image," *Liturgy with a Difference*, xiv.

6. Richard R. Gaillardetz, "Ecclesial Belonging in This Time of Scandal," *Worship* 94 (July 2020): 204.

of ten Catholics attend Mass each week,[7] it is all the more important that hospitality and welcome be extended in a renewed approach to ecumenism. Perhaps the downward trend in interest in Sunday Mass (although not an excuse to remove it from the top priorities of Catholics) provides an opportunity to promote Christian engagement with the wider world with an ecumenical focus. Having pronounced that "the restoration of unity among all Christians is one of the principal concerns of the Second Vatican Council,"[8] the Council Fathers described the spirit of ecumenism as follows:

> Before the whole world let all Christians confess their faith in God, one and three, in the incarnate Son of God, our Redeemer and Lord. United in their efforts, and with mutual respect, let them bear witness to our common hope which does not play us false. Since cooperation in social matters is so widespread today, all people without exception are called to work together; with much greater reason is this true of all who believe in God, but most of all, it is especially true of all Christians, since they bear the seal of Christ's name. Cooperation among Christians vividly expresses that bond which already unites them, and it sets in clearer relief the features of Christ the Servant.[9]

It has taken some time since the Second Vatican Council for Catholics to truly embrace the words in Ephesians: "one body and one Spirit, as you were also called to the one hope of your call; one Lord, one faith, one baptism" (4:4–5). Many continue to believe that being baptized in the Catholic Church is somehow better than being baptized in a Methodist or a Lutheran community. However, such thinking is disappearing as Catholics and other Christians cooperate in so many activities outside

---

7. Gallup, "Catholics' Church Attendance Resumes Downward Slide," (April 9, 2018). https://news.gallup.com/poll/232226/church-attendance-among-catholics-resumes-downward-slide.aspx.

8. *Decree on Ecumenism* (*Unitatis redintegratio* [UR]), 1.

9. UR, 12.

religion and, in common faith-based undertakings, demonstrate great cooperation. It is necessary that our parish leaders continue the work of ecumenism. In ministries that involve the youth, it is particularly important that Christians of different denominations learn from each other and that respect for our one baptism continues to grow.

In so many ways, all of the points discussed on how leading through our baptism can bring about the transformation of our parish communities can be summed up in the understanding that baptism into Christ involves participation in the paschal mystery. It is so easy to say that the central mystery of our faith is the paschal mystery, but do we truly understand what this demands? The general introduction to *Christian Initiation* (CI) states: "Those who are baptized are united with Christ in a death like his, are buried with him in death, and also in him are given life and are raised up."[10] Two components of this statement are key: we are called to a death like Christ's, and we rise to new life again. Taking the first component, Jesus offered his life as a sacrifice of love to the Father—that is the beauty of the cross. Our Christian lives are to embody a sacrificial nature. Second, Jesus' resurrection to new life destroys the darkness of death. For us, this means that no sin, suffering, or sadness should conquer our ability to hope for a new day. Ultimately, the most important fact about the paschal mystery is that the death and resurrection was not about Jesus but about his love for others. Baptism is about shifting the focus from ourselves to others; it is about seeing God's love as gift not for me alone but as tangibly alive for everyone as God builds up the unity of a diverse world. Mary A. Ehle beautifully writes:

But ultimately, the most important fact about the paschal mystery is that the death and resurrection was not about Jesus but about his love for others.

---

10. *Christian Initiation*, 6.

In a divided world, God's embrace of love at Baptism charges us with the responsibility to help bring about unity in the world while still respecting the marvelous, creative differences in everyone whom God has created. Asking ourselves how we can offer God's embrace of love to people in a world where many find themselves polarized from others politically, economically, socially, culturally, ethnically, and religiously is a question we must ask. The words and deeds of a Christian must serve to build unity in a diverse world that at its best is a reflection of the amazing love the three Divine Persons in the unity of God offers to us.[11]

It has been said that one of the most dangerous heresies ever to invade Christianity was the idea that faith is about an individual relationship with God that can be lived neatly and privately. The truth is that Christianity is far from neat and definitely not private. Christianity involves death to self for the world. Death involves the struggle of letting go and recognizing one's lack of self-sufficiency. It is necessarily messy. In

Our participation in the paschal mystery is meant to be for the salvation of the world, neither directed toward ourselves nor disguised in neat and tidy packaging.

our culture, we tend to disguise death and to avoid pain. Rather than embracing the lot of suffering, we want a quick fix. Our baptism asks us to approach life from the worldview of the Suffering Servant, who refuses to shirk the suffering imposed on him by the world and, by depending upon the Father, transforms it into glory. Our participation in the paschal mystery is meant to be for the salvation of the world, neither directed toward ourselves nor disguised in neat and tidy packaging.

Our common baptism entails walking with others and thus involves leadership. While Christ is always before us, we are meant to

---

11. Mary A. Ehle, *Anointed for Discipleship: The Meaning of Baptism for Our Christian Life* (Chicago: Liturgy Training Publications, 2019, 2022), 9.

share in the responsibility of coming together in service. Therefore, we contemplate two images of leadership that are biblical and suggest how we might lead together.

The first image is that of the Good Shepherd from the tenth chapter of John's Gospel. Jesus proclaims himself to be the Good Shepherd, who "lays down his life for his sheep" (10:11), who knows his sheep and his sheep know him (10:14), who has sheep from other flocks (10:16), and whose voice will be heard and followed by all because "there will be one flock, one shepherd" (10:17). A bond of unity exists between the Good Shepherd and the sheep because the Shepherd roots his life in the sheep's, knowing their struggles, experiencing their pain. Leading through our baptism requires a willingness to become immersed in the lives of others. Pope Francis contends that evangelization is accomplished today when leaders "smell like the sheep." He writes in *Evangelii gaudium (The Joy of the Gospel* [EG]):

> An evangelizing community gets involved by word and deed in people's daily lives; it bridges distances, it is willing to abase itself if necessary, and it embraces human life, touching the suffering flesh of Christ in others. Evangelizers thus take on the "smell of the sheep" and the sheep are willing to hear their voice. An evangelizing community is also supportive, standing by people at every step of the way, no matter how difficult or lengthy this may prove to be. It is familiar with patient expectation and apostolic endurance. Evangelization consists mostly of patience and disregard for constraints of time.[12]

Applying this image of the "smell of the sheep" to the leadership of priests, Cardinal Donald Wuerl asserts that the challenge is for leadership to be out amongst the people: "The priest cannot shepherd the flock from afar, he must be there with people in their journey. He must walk

---

12. EG, 24.

with them, side-by-side."[13] Baptism does not separate us from the world but immerses us ever deeper into its beating heartbeat bestowed with the gift of God's mercy to share. Discipleship requires an active and prayerful listening to the Shepherd, the Head of the Body. Everything about the Good Shepherd embodies a servant attitude to leadership. To follow, we embrace the very same sacrificial spirit.

If Jesus is the Good Shepherd who leads and guards his flock day and night, a corresponding image most fitting for the Church is the title "a pilgrim people." Pilgrimage necessitates the abandonment of self-focus and a willingness to live in the moment. A pilgrim is one who lives in a sort of in-between space—neither here nor there—always seeking to move into the horizon. As Kevin Codd writes, "Life's difficult passages, sorrows, crosses, even deaths necessarily lead to new life in all kinds of surprising and glorious ways. Keeping an eye peeled for grace ahead guards us from despair. . . . We fall, we fail, we harm one another. Then we rise, we reconcile, we heal, and we continue down the road."[14] The pilgrim way embraces life as an ongoing process. Even when the pilgrim reaches the so-called endpoint, his or her pilgrimage is not over; it has just begun. So it is with our baptismal life. Each day is a choice to live as a disciple of Christ—to pick up, to heal, and to start anew.

When called a "pilgrim people," the Church is often mistakenly viewed as being impatient for heaven, striving to get through this life as quickly as possible. However, real pilgrimage is about living in the present, which means that grace is found in the journey itself. As previously discussed, corporate discernment on the part of the baptized is not meant to be far-reaching. Instead, it is meant to discern God's will for us at this very moment. The better we are at discerning the gifts of all

---

13. See Mark Zimmerman, "Pope Wants Priests to Be Shepherds Who Encounter Their Flocks," *Crux* (June 16, 2017), https://cruxnow.com/vatican/2017/06/pope -wants-priests-shepherds-encounter-flocks.

14. Kevin A. Codd, " 'I Am a Pilgrim on the Earth': The Pilgrim Way," *Worship* 84 (2010): 169.

the members of the Body and the more courageous we are in calling upon the members to use their gifts for the good of all, the greater will be our ability to recognize the healing power of God's grace at every step of our pilgrim journey. Words from *Lumen gentium* close our reflection on baptism as transforming Christian community:

> All the members must be formed in his likeness, until Christ is formed in them (see Galatians 4:19). . . . On earth, still as pilgrims in a strange land, following in trial and in oppression the paths he trod, we are associated with his sufferings as the body with its head, suffering with him, that with him we may be glorified (see Romans 8:17). . . . From him "the whole body, supplied and built up by joints and ligaments, attains a growth that is of God" (Colossians 2:19). He constantly makes available in his body, which is the church, gifts of ministries through which, by his power, we provide each other with the helps needed for salvation so that, doing the truth in love, we may in all things grow into him who is our head (see Ephesians 4:11–16, Greek). [15]

The Good Shepherd leads us on our pilgrim way, a journey that begins in our baptism and continues to unfold in our baptism until all creation is knit together as one in life eternal.

❖ Discussion Questions ❖

1. When have you changed your approach or decision because you listened to others?

2. Have you ever noticed a difference in the way you might listen to someone based on their gender, race, ethnicity, or degree of participation in the parish?

3. How can the parish staff show parishioners who rarely attend the liturgy that they are valued and that their input is desired?

---

15. LG, 7.

4. Does an understanding that grace is found in the journey help you put aside time constraints in listening to God and others?

5. How might the staff assist parishioners in working toward unity and not just toward the goals of their parish organization or committee?

PART 2

CALLING THE PARISH TO ITS BAPTISMAL VOCATION

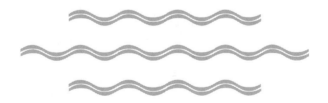

CHAPTER 4

The Door to Life and to the Kingdom

Amen, amen, I say to you, no one can enter the kingdom of God without being born of water and Spirit. What is born of flesh is flesh and what is born of spirit is spirit.

—John 3:5–6

In the context of the rich imagery Jesus employs in identifying himself as the Good Shepherd in the tenth chapter of John's Gospel is the statement: "I am the gate for the sheep" (10:7). While Jesus contends that the sheep know him, listen to his voice, and follow him (10:27), he also proposes that he is the "gate" through which his followers must pass in order to find pasture. A gate?

A gate, or a door, provides several functions. First, the threshold of a door can be considered a liminal space that calls for a choice. When a person stands in a doorway, he or she is neither in the interior or the exterior space; instead, the person is in between. Thus, in a very real sense, a gate is a place of discernment. One has to weigh the consequences of entering versus remaining outside. Second, as a passageway, the door provides a means of identification. One who has passed through the gate into the space that lies beyond may be considered to belong to that new location. As anthropologist Arnold van Gennep writes: "The door is the boundary between the foreign and domestic worlds in the case of an ordinary dwelling. . . . Therefore, to cross the threshold is to unite oneself with a new world."[1] Finally, a door provides a means of safety for those inside. If the door is well fortified and locked, it prevents outsiders from gaining entrance and protects those insiders from wandering away. Jesus states: "I am the gate. Whoever enters by me will be saved, and will come in and go out and find pasture" (John 10:9).

Like a gate, baptism involves (1) discerning a new way of life, (2) making the decision to cross over into a new world, and (3) discovering the security of freedom in Christ. Baptism initiates a Christian in the way of the paschal mystery and thus invites followers to put on a "paschal" approach to life. This means looking at death to self as the way to resurrected life, for in baptism, one must pass through death to self to belong fully to Christ. Thus, it is quite natural that the Church would understand baptism as the sacrament that provides entrance into Christ. It is the door through which an individual makes a choice to enter, discovers a new identity on the other side, and finds safety and security in the way of life Jesus offers. Canon 849 of the *Code of Canon Law* defines baptism as follows:

> Baptism, the gateway to the sacraments and necessary for salvation by actual reception or at least by desire, is validly conferred only by a washing of true water with the proper form of words. Through baptism men and women are freed from sin, are reborn as children of God, and, configured to Christ by an indelible character, are incorporated into the Church.[2]

While there is a fair amount of legality in this definition of baptism, such as the requirements of "true water" and the "form of words," the theology contained within is rich. Baptism provides an "indelible character" that cannot be stripped away as well as real "incorporation" into

---

1. Arnold van Gennep, *The Rites of Passage* (Chicago: University of Chicago Press, 1960), 20.
2. Canon 849.

the Church that continues on into the heavenly realm. Baptism provides identity and entrance. Once a person has been grafted onto Christ in baptism, theirs is a new world that cannot be abandoned.

Ponder for a moment the placement of the baptismal font in a church. Ancient baptisteries constructed for the immersion of adult men and women were usually built as separate rooms very near the entrance of the worship space. The symbolic meaning of this placement is clear: one must pass through the waters of baptism to participate in the new life that lies within the community of Jesus' followers. However, as adult initiation waned in practice and medieval superstition resulted in the need to lock up the powers of holy water, pools at the entrance of the church gradually became small stoops placed near the altar, allowing for a minimal amount of movement on the part of the priest. Even when baptismal fonts are located in areas within the church building other than at the door, the waters of baptism continue to symbolize immersion into the new and exciting life that is adventure with Christ, or discipleship.

Not only does the baptismal font play a significant role in welcoming new members into Christ as well as reminding the baptized of their Christian duties, but the door itself plays an important role in marking life in Christ. Think about all the liturgical rites that the door silently witnesses. The *Order of Celebrating Matrimony* suggests that the liturgy begin with the priest greeting the couple at the door and that they process together to the altar. At the outset of the funeral liturgy, the priest welcomes the body of the deceased as well as the family at the door of the church, and there sprinkles the casket with water and covers it with the pall, all done in remembrance of the moment the person first entered the church through the sacrament of baptism. Thus, it is ideal when we witness infant baptisms starting at the church door with the minister greeting the family and requesting the name of the child to be baptized. Similarly, the *Rite of Christian Initiation of Adults* envisions the rite of acceptance into the order of catechumens opening as "the candidates, their sponsors, and a group of the faithful gather outside the church" to clearly designate this ritual as the moment of "entrance" into the faith journey.[3]

If a door clearly marks a place of discernment and new identity, then what about the aspect of security? Doors and gates are designed to protect. They keep out what is not welcomed and keep in what is to remain. Therefore, gates can be either hospitable or unwelcoming. If Christ is "the gate," every door of the church—those of our church buildings and those of our hearts—must be hospitable. The United States Conference of Catholic Bishops' document *Disciples Called to Witness: The New Evangelization* invites each parish to reimagine everything it is and does as being about the work of evangelization. At the forefront of evangelization is a hospitable welcome, for as *Disciples Called to Witness* states: "The entire parish community, especially the parish leadership, must foster a spirit of hospitality and welcome."[4] Furthermore, the document suggests that opening the door in welcome is constituted simply in the visible living of a corporate, Christian lifestyle:

> To create a culture of witness, we must live explicit lives of discipleship. Being a disciple is a challenge. Fortunately, one does not become a disciple on his or her own initiative. The work of the Holy Spirit within the Christian community forms the person as a disciple of Christ. . . .
>
> The commitment to living the Christian life provides an essential element of the culture of witness. To those seeking answers to the increasing secularization, individualism, and materialism of society, a Christian life provides a powerful witness to the Gospel. The public profession of one's faith through active participation in prayer,

---

3. RCIA, 48.

4. *Disciples Called to Witness: The New Evangelization* (Washington, DC: United States Conference of Catholic Bishops, 2012), 17.

the sacraments, and especially Sunday Mass contributes to the sanctification of the world. Additionally, the works of charity and justice as well as the promotion of solidarity, justice, peace and stewardship of creation build up the Kingdom of God.[5]

Thus, leadership within the parish that is based on baptism is focused on the attitude of hospitality. The Gospel bears witness to the fact that Jesus did not understand his ministry to usher in the kingdom of God to be about setting up shop in Galilee, with the expectation that people would come to him. Instead, he ventured out into the highways and byways, and welcomed people into the mystery of God's kingdom. His miracles of reconciliation and healing were most often done when he detected a glimpse of faith residing in the needy person. He must have believed that a simple act of compassion and love on his part would ignite real transformation in the hearts of those he encountered.

Jesus did not understand his ministry to usher in the kingdom of God to be about setting up shop in Galilee, with the expectation that people would come to him.

Leaders within the parish must be men and women who have the same hope for acts of hospitality today. A parish must be built up around the expectation that every member is called to be a hospitable representative of Christ and that every member see himself or herself as doing the work of evangelization, the task of every disciple. The introduction to the *Rite of Christian Initiation of Adults* (RCIA) states: "The people of God, as represented by the local Church, should understand and show by their concern that the initiation of adults is the responsibility of all the baptized. Therefore, the community must always be fully prepared in the pursuit of its apostolic vocation to give help to those who are searching for Christ."[6] In reality, so much of providing a welcome in our

---

5. *Disciples Called to Witness*, 11–12.

6. RCIA, 9.

parishes is about revealing the servant attitude of Christ, seeking to give up ourselves in the service of God's kingdom. All who are baptized into Christ participate in keeping watch over the gate. It is hoped that those who pass through it will experience within the true freedom Christ promises.

❧ Pastoral Reflections ❧

Religious Educator
Cristina Castillo

Faith formation leaders serve as the point of welcome for families and individuals seeking formation in the faith. Many times, those overseeing any or all faith formation programs are seen as gatekeepers of the faith. As we stand at the gate, we must be ready to act upon our call to be witnesses for Christ. The gatekeepers should serve as ushers as people arrive at the door. Too many times, those in leadership become gatekeepers who never open the gates. As a result, families or individuals are turned away.

Emmanuel, a single father, was told his daughters could not continue their first Communion classes because of a pending balance from year one. Instead of continuing to plead his case at his home parish, Emmanuel traveled a few more blocks and arrived at my parish. I offered him the opportunity to volunteer in the religious education office. Emmanuel helped with the classroom setup on Sundays, and he also helped with our fundraisers. I chose to assist him because the same had been done for my mom when she couldn't pay for our registration for first Communion or confirmation.

> As we stand at the gate, we must be ready to act upon our call to be witnesses for Christ.

Our leadership roles are crucial and even more so when we have individuals returning to their faith. Unfortunately, many people find judgment instead of welcome. For example, let us look at Julian, a young adult who spent years being angry at God. He became mad at God after he prayed for his mom, and she still died. Now, he has come back to his parish to help with livestreaming Masses. As he approaches an extraordinary minister of holy Communion, he is told, "You were not present during Mass. Therefore, you are unable to receive." He explains that he was managing the livestreaming, yet he is turned away. Julian continued returning to help his parish, but many others would have left for good or would have looked for a new parish. When we offer solutions or opportunities for people, we show we care for the person. The same applies to any ministry within a parish.

Music Minister
Michael Conrady

As a director of music for more than twenty-five years, my work has allowed me to serve God, help others, work in a creative field, and meet amazing people.

Yet there have been times when ministry was not easy. When I first made the leap of faith to pursue a career in ministry, I left behind a promising career in business. Soon, I was surprised by the difficulty of the transition, as I became immersed in hard work, long hours, and a steep learning curve. As sometimes happens to young people in ministry, I had accepted a role that was too large for one person. As a result, I found myself in situations where I felt overwhelmed. Numerous times I wanted to go back to my former life.

But though my initial role was challenging, I was in a parish that helped me learn about ministry. My pastor was an experienced priest who taught me a tremendous amount about liturgy and music. I inherited well-organized, thriving ministries led by people who were eager to bring me up to speed. Many of the friends I made during that period have turned into lifelong friends.

Through the challenges, I grew in discipline, knowledge, and faith. I learned how to prioritize work. I learned how to respond to people in a pastoral way. And in those moments when I felt like I was drowning, the Lord was teaching me to put my trust in him. I didn't know it at the time, but God was using the challenges to prepare me for larger projects and responsibilities.

During that time, I learned to embrace my calling and recognize God's plan in my life. The author of the eighteenth-century hymn "How Firm a Foundation" may have known that comfort when he penned:

When through the deep waters I call you to go
The rivers of sorrow shall not overflow

For I will be with you, your troubles to bless
And sanctify to you your deepest distress.

If we expect to participate in the death and resurrection of the Lord, then our act of dying to self will consist of real sacrifice. Although the challenges of ministry can seem overwhelming at times, personal and spiritual growth usually follow these periods. Not all growth is pleasant, but the promises of the Lord are everlasting.

Volunteer Coordinator
Caroline Okello

> Those who enter the font, whether they be mature adults or newborn infants, embark upon a completely new way of life that is, simply put, "life with Christ." (Page 4 of this book.)

Guided by the Holy Spirit, I requested to be baptized when I was ten years old. I am from a developing nation, where very little is known of Christianity, let alone Catholicism. The fourth child in a family of seven children, I was born to a Catholic father and a non-Catholic mother. My three older siblings were baptized in infancy, but my younger siblings and I were not.

When I was nine years old, I got involved in the choir at the basilica nearby where my father often took us for Mass. It was an all-adult choir, but they welcomed me. I was assigned to play *kayamba*, an African instrument which I developed a great love for. To this day, when I see a kayamba anywhere, I always want to pick it up and play.

My love for the faith grew and I was determined to receive Communion. When I researched what it would take to achieve that goal, I found that I needed to be baptized, and to do that I must go through catechism. Because I wanted to receive Communion so badly, I was ready to start catechism immediately, but there was another requirement: parental consent. Permission was granted and I went through catechism, was baptized, and received my first holy Communion on the same day. Even though I was the fourth member of my family to be baptized, I became the first to receive holy Communion.

From that day, I never looked back. Even though I was already involved in the music ministry in the parish, my true discipleship started with my baptism. My determination to celebrate the sacraments inspired my siblings, both older and younger, to do the same. Also, through my baptism, my father returned to the Church after having lapsed in his attendance for some years. My mother, too, was inspired and went through the Christian initiation process and was received into the Catholic Church.

Sometimes we lead others to faith without even knowing how. We don't realize when the Spirit is working through us, but looking back, we can see the Spirit at work in our lives. Fortunately, one does not become a disciple on his or her own initiative. The work of the Holy Spirit within the Christian community forms the person as a disciple of Christ. (*Disciples Called to Witness*, 17)

Pastor
Father Patrick A. Smith

When I was a toddler in the 1960s, my family moved from one part of Washington, DC, to another. Upon making this move from Holy Redeemer Parish to St. Francis Xavier Parish, my parents did something that is rare in some urban areas today: they changed their parish registration and withdrew their children—four of my older siblings—from the old parish school and placed them in the new one. My parents attended the church within the parish boundaries of their new home. This sense of duty to attend your geographically located parish is often overlooked in many areas of the country now. People often opt to be part of parishes where they feel welcome and their spirits are nurtured.

For me, the key has been to present the parish as a community in mission; a mission that began with our baptism.

This has certainly been my experience in parishes where I have served as the pastor, including at my current parish. With over 2,500 households, St. Augustine is a big parish in Washington, DC. In this city, people have many options for where to spend their Sunday mornings worshiping; almost as many options as to where to spend their Sunday brunches eating. That's one of my biggest challenges as a pastor. How do I get parishioners to not reduce the parish to a spiritual restaurant—a place to be fed and served only? Stephen S. Wilbricht, csc, states, "Jesus did not understand his ministry to usher in the kingdom of God to be about setting up shop in Galilee, with the expectation that people would come to him. Instead, he ventured out into the highways and byways" (page 47).

For me, the key has been to present the parish as a community in mission, a mission that began with our baptism: "A parish must be built up around the expectation that every member is called to be a hospitable representative of Christ and that every member see himself or herself as doing the work of evangelization" (page 47).

The idea of parish boundaries, as understood in my parents' day, may seem obsolete in modern times, but this is not necessarily true. The difference today may be a matter of focus. Rather than parish boundaries informing Catholics where they are supposed to go to church, today they tell the Church where it's supposed to go!

❖ Discussion Questions ❖

1. While acting as welcoming gatekeepers, how can we be creative in finding ways to assist people to live out their baptismal responsibilities?

2. How will we encourage liturgical ministers and other parish leaders to die to self as they put aside judgmental attitudes and accompany others as gatekeepers?

3. Are members of the parish staff looking out for people enthusiastic in their faith, such as Caroline Okello, so that their faith will be nurtured?

4. How can the parish team support each other during challenges that require dying to self so that we may rise in Christ?

5. What can we do to help our parishioners realize that the parish is a community in mission, that all are to become gatekeepers, going outside the parish boundaries to welcome people and evangelize?

PRAYER

Hymn Suggestion:

"God Has Chosen Me," Bernadette Farrell, OCP Publications Inc., 1990.

Reading   (Mark 4:26–32)

He [Jesus] said, "This is how it is with the kingdom of God; it is as if a man were to scatter seed on the land and would sleep and rise night and day and the seed would sprout and grow, he knows not how. Of its own accord the land yields fruit, first the blade, then the ear, then the full grain in the ear. And when the grain is ripe, he wields the sickle at once, for the harvest has come."

He said, "To what shall we compare the kingdom of God, or what parables can we use for it? It is like a mustard seed that, when it is sown in the ground is the smallest of all the seeds on the earth. But once it is sown, it springs up and becomes the largest of plants and puts forth large branches, so that the birds of the sky can dwell in its shade."

> ### ❧ Reflection ❧
>
> Farmers must be attentive to nature and the proper time for planting and must patiently await the appearance of new life. The first sight of seedlings certainly brings great joy. So it is with the seeds of faith that are planted at baptism. The sacrament of baptism opens the door to the kingdom of God. It also opens the way to the adventure of living with Christ as disciples. Even though we trust in the growth of God's kingdom, it remains largely a mystery to us—we do not know precisely what makes it bud forth. Our task is to be observant disciples, who actively wait with patience, labor with love, and rejoice at the sight of new growth.

Prayer of the Faithful

Looking to the Lord, who first loved us, we pray:

✳ That the preaching of the Church may sow the seeds of the kingdom deep within the hearts of all who hear, we pray: **Lord, hear our prayer.**

✳ That the nations of this world may use the natural resources of our planet with prudence and care, we pray: **Lord, hear our prayer.**

✳ That all who earn their living by working the land may be observant stewards of nature's gifts, we pray: **Lord, hear our prayer.**

✳ That zeal for the coming of God's kingdom may grow and develop in the hearts of all the baptized, we pray: **Lord, hear our prayer.**

✳ That the dead may be raised to new and eternal life, we pray: **Lord, hear our prayer.**

Gathering these petitions, let us pray as the Lord taught us:

Our Father . . .

Collect

> Almighty God,
> we give you thanks for the wonders of creation.
> Everywhere we look
> we see the seedlings of your kingdom.
> May those baptized as followers of your Son
> be good and prudent stewards
> of all that you have created
> and work together for that perfect day
> when we will pass through the door to life eternal.
> Through Christ our Lord.
> Amen.

CHAPTER 5

Built Up Together into a Dwelling Place of God

As a body is one though it has many parts, and all the parts of the
body, though many, are one body, so also Christ. For in one Spirit
we were all baptized into one body, whether Jews or Greeks, slaves
or free persons, and we were all given to drink of one Spirit.

—1 Corinthians 12:12–13

For far too many of the centuries of Christianity, the sacrament of
baptism was celebrated as a private affair, mostly with the understanding that it is necessary for the washing away of original sin and for
making possible eternal life with God. Fortunately, the liturgical renewal
ushered in by the Second Vatican Council called for the retrieval of the
ecclesial nature of the sacrament. Baptism is not simply about the salvation of an individual soul, it is about entrance into the Church and
corporate participation with all the members of the Body of Christ.
The general introduction to *Christian Initiation* states quite clearly
that "baptism is the Sacrament by which human beings are incorporated
into the Church and are built up together into a dwelling place of God
in the Spirit."[1]

---

1. CI, 4.

Recapturing the communal nature of the sacrament helps underscore a renewed understanding of sacramental grace. Grace is not something that we receive that can be saved up to demonstrate personal righteousness; instead, grace is union with God bestowed in Christ that is to be rediscovered daily. Prior to the conciliar renewal, the enactment of baptism, in which an infant was christened in the presence of godparents (and sometimes the child's parents) alone, highlighted an almost magical understanding of baptism, whereby the new Christian would be welcomed into heaven by God, no questions asked. However, when a child's baptism is celebrated in the context of a true Christian assembly, it becomes quite clear that grace involves active participation. God is willing to work with us, but we must be willing to work as well . . . *together*!

The obligation to participate in regular liturgical celebration is not for the purpose of individual Christians to prove themselves to be faithful to God as much as it is for Christians to come together to learn how to function as one holy people. It is said often that all liturgy has at its core the remembering of the paschal mystery, or the suffering, death, and resurrection of Jesus. However, it is seldom understood that remembering the paschal mystery means that individual wor-

In other words, the prayer of the Church is not a collection of individuals praying for their particular needs, but a *body* that strives to recognize its oneness in Christ.

shipers must work to surrender themselves by allowing themselves to be reincorporated deeper and deeper into the worshiping assembly. In other words, the prayer of the Church is not a collection of individuals praying for their particular needs, but a *body* that strives to recognize its oneness in Christ. Praying together ought to help us discern the particular charisms that each member of the Body of Christ offers for the building up of the entire Church. Mark Searle likens such corporate prayer of attentiveness to the working of God's justice, writing:

For the members of the worshiping community, relationships with one's fellow human beings are based not simply upon their common humanity but upon their common humanity as assumed and redeemed by the love and obedience of Jesus, and raised to a new level by the Spirit of Jesus at work in the world. . . . The liturgical assembly, at least in its ideal form, offers a model of such interaction. It is not a community of equals but a community of God-given and complementary charisms, gifts that cannot be identified *a priori* by categories of the secular community—age, sex, race—but are distributed indiscriminately among all for the sole purpose of building up the community in perfect justice.[2]

When the Spirit gathers the liturgical assembly to be re-membered in Christ (or to be put back together again in the risen Lord), the common worship is meant to fine tune the worldview of its participants, so that they learn to see the world as Christ sees it. In Searle's words, the liturgy "presupposes a group of people who can reach across the social, political, and economic barriers that structure our world to say 'Our Father' and to speak of themselves as a 'we.'"[3]

If baptism incorporates new members into the Body of Christ, then the living of daily life for each member, with experiences of joy and sorrow, accomplishments and defeats, requires that relationships get put back together in new and different ways to pursue unity. Thus, parish leadership must work to guarantee that worship is a priority of the community, together with an understanding that liturgy is about all of us together, working hard to see how Christ is refashioning us anew as his Body. Again, the words of Mark Searle:

The liturgy is a rehearsal of the roles we are called to take upon ourselves throughout life. We are to become what we are. The liturgy puts us into the position we are called to adopt, and week by week

---

2. Mark Searle, "Serving the Lord with Justice," in *Liturgy and Social Justice*, ed. Mark Searle (Collegeville, MN: Liturgical Press, 1980), 24.

3. Searle, "Serving the Lord with Justice," 25.

rehearses us in our parts as members of the one Body. If we were already perfect, if we had our parts down pat, we would not need the rehearsal: The whole of life would be a celebration of Eucharist, a realization of our identity as the reconciled People of God. But rehearse we must, and each part of the liturgy is part of the vision of peace and a rehearsal of our roles as peacemakers.[4]

Consider, for example, the simple illustration of the assembly's procession during Communion. How does the liturgy rehearse us to see this liturgical gesture in a more profound light than simply the need for people to get to the altar to receive Communion? Searle would argue that part of the responsibility of the baptized to participate fully and consciously in the liturgy would be to contemplate this gesture to behold the presence of Christ. Observing the people processing toward the altar may result in an act of judgment, whereby I critique the attire or the worthiness of individual communicants. Or it could involve the suspension of judgment and the contemplative work of discerning Christ, whereby each individual, unique communicant, as part of a diverse array of ages and incomes, colors and lifestyle, worries and needs, forms the Body of Christ, rehearsing that day when all the nations will gather in praise around the throne of God. According to Searle, the liturgical action of Communion is how the Church learns a way of life that is about "giving" and "taking." "The Eucharist," writes Searle, "is the sacrament of giving and taking in the community of Christ's Body, which is the Church. . . . One bread broken and shared; one cup poured out and passed around; one people giving and taking. Not eating in private; not self-service, but feasting in common: hand in hand, person to person, all for one and one for all, given and taken."[5]

---

4. Mark Searle, "Grant Us Peace . . . Do We Hear What We Are Saying?" This article, most likely written in the early 1980s, is reproduced as appendix 2 in my book, *Rehearsing God's Just Kingdom: The Eucharistic Vision of Mark Searle* (Collegeville, MN: 2013), 215–227. The quote appears on page 223. This is the first time the article appears in a published source.

5. Mark Searle, "The Act of Communion: A Commentary," *Assembly* (1978): 6.

Another way in which the liturgy helps in forming relationships according to baptismal commitments is in the enactment of the collection. Parish finances are a concern for nearly every pastor. They most likely welcome the idea of replacing the Sunday collection with a direct deposit system. Such a plan is convenient for pastors who count on a regular flow of income and parishioners who then do not need to worry about writing a check or using an envelope. While seemingly a grand idea for fiscal management, the direct deposit system strips the collection of its liturgical significance. In its origins, the collection was the moment for a profound redistribution of wealth, whereby those who had plenty shared what they had with others *for the good of the entire community*. Members of the assembly would witness people bringing articles of clothing, produce from their gardens, and animals from their folds that they wanted to give to the poor.

By and large, we are greatly removed from the vision of the Eucharist as the place where wealth is redistributed for members of the Body of Christ to enact and celebrate their unity. But such a widespread deprivation ought to summon us to make our assemblies places where justice is realized. What are we doing to visibly connect our worship to our baptismal obligation to work for God's just kingdom? In her book, *The Meal That Reconnects: Eucharistic Eating and the Global Food Crisis*, Mary McGann argues that as people make their way through the doors of any church building, they ought to be able to detect the presence of a community concerned for the needs of the poor and of the world. She describes an innovation by a community to use an empty lot as a garden to feed the hungry:

A community in western Canada has transformed a vacant lot beside the church into a permaculture garden where members toil to raise fruits and vegetables for local food pantries. Passing through this colorful and fragrant expression of God's creation on Sunday morning—and occasionally gathering there for opening rites—

members are often met by neighbors who contribute daily to the work of the garden and who wish to join them for Sunday worship.[6]

Thus, the planting of a garden on the parish grounds is a creative way that allows people to imaginatively connect the celebration of the paschal mystery within the liturgy with the realization of the paschal mystery in daily life. The planting and maintaining of a garden demand hard work on the part of disciples who are willing to sacrifice themselves so that others in the community might live.

So it is with all of our liturgical worship. We are gathered by the Holy Spirit to be built up into the dwelling place of God. All that we do in liturgy is about discovering ever deeper the bonds of unity that we share in Christ. The faithful rehearse many roles within the liturgical body to be sent forth into the world

All that we do in liturgy is about discovering ever deeper the bonds of unity that we share in Christ.

as the reconciled Body of Christ, prepared to invite others into the mystery of the kingdom. For this very reason, we are sent forth from liturgical prayer, not as individuals but as one Church: "Go in peace, glorifying the Lord by your life."

❧ Pastoral Reflections ❦

Religious Educator
Cristina Castillo

My first role as a minister came at the age of seven, altar serving. One of my first lessons, "You are to become invisible and be one with the candle." A lesson I have passed on to others. Candlebearers focus on the light from the flame and allow the light to shine and to guide the assembly to each part of the liturgy. They participate as they are attentive and pray and sing with the assembled. For me, altar serving was about disappearing behind

---

6. Mary E. McGann, *The Meal That Reconnects: Eucharistic Eating and the Global Food Crisis* (Collegeville, MN: Liturgical Press, 2020), 156.

the candle and letting the candle shine brightly as all gather as one to celebrate and recall the paschal mystery each Sunday.

In the sacrament of baptism, we are anointed as priests, prophets, and kings. Same as when Jesus was baptized and anointed. The baptized are called to be greater than themselves. As part of the leadership, we must instill these teachings in the current and future leaders of the Church. The liturgy is rich in teaching, and when the community is taught the meaning of the celebration of the Eucharist, we become active participants rather than spectators. The priest isn't the only one offering the Mass. All of the assembly actively participates and offers the Mass together as one Body of Christ.

As we gather to celebrate the Eucharist as one, we offer up our communal gifts throughout Mass. The communal nature of the liturgy makes it the appropriate place for the celebration of the sacraments. For example, baptism is the Christian initiation of an infant (or adult), and they should be welcomed into the Catholic family by the community members. Together we rejoice and celebrate the initiation of the new member. When a sacrament is celebrated in private, the communal sense of the celebration is lost. Just as a birthday is celebrated in the midst of our community of family and friends, sacraments are celebrated in the midst of the faith community. We commit ourselves to guide each other in our faith journey. We become active witnesses in each other's lives to ensure we proclaim the good news to all.

Music Minister   Michael Conrady

A great deal of the work and energy that pastoral musicians put into each rehearsal is related to technical matters. In preparation for each liturgy, music ministers make countless refinements as they hone diction, rhythms, intonation, dynamics, phrasing, and so on. Sometimes the work can be tedious, not unlike that of a sculptor who whittles away excess material to reveal a figure. The result of all our efforts is a carefully crafted piece of music.

But it would be a mistake to consider this music as our sole contribution. The music we create is an essential and beautiful part of the liturgy. But in the process of creating music, we minister to each other. When we gather as baptized Christians, something special happens. In the sharing of our music, our faith is shared. As we pray and sing together, our deepest hopes and dreams are shared. As we recount our daily struggles, the good news of what God is doing in our lives is shared.

When a choir member or musician, then, asks to speak with me after a rehearsal or Mass, I know the conversation will probably not be about diction, rhythms, or intonation. Usually, they need to talk about a challenge they are facing. Occasionally we celebrate joys, but more often, we talk candidly about struggles with faith, physical illness, family, employment, or mental health. I listen and sometimes I pray and offer encouragement. When needed, I connect them with resources and other support. I

> Through my baptism, I serve the people of God who trust me to walk alongside them, help share their daily burdens, and offer support and prayer.

am not ordained, but through my baptism, I serve the people of God who trust me to walk alongside them, help share their daily burdens, and offer support and prayer. This is not a part of my ministry that people see. For all the world, I work with talented people to create beautiful works of art for the community. But this hidden work is the most precious to me.

Volunteer Coordinator   Caroline Okello

When Masses were allowed to resume during the COVID-19 pandemic, I was hired as the parish's welcome and volunteer coordinator. In this newly created position, I took charge of the COVID-related arrangements for Mass—assisting with the registration process and preparing the seating in the church for each liturgy, based on the number of families and the number of people within each family. The team I formed assisted with checking people in and escorting them to their seats. Soon, I noticed that parishioners were quick to offer feedback, whether with suggestions to improve our system or to affirm how safe they feel attending Mass at our parish.

The pandemic disrupted our norms. For many Catholics, the norm is to sit in the same spot in church, week after week, in some cases year after year. One person slammed his walker at me to make his point as he told me that he has sat in the same spot for fifty years and he did not want to sit anywhere else. It took time for him to adapt, but my team was patient and eventually he accepted the pandemic guidelines as the new normal, and became one of the sweetest people, with the utmost respect for the hospitality team.

Not too long after starting this job, I mastered many of our parishioners' names, and began to call them by their first names as I checked them in during registration. Astonished that I knew him by name, one congregant approached me with a broad smile that I saw in his eyes despite his mask, saying, "You know my name?!" It was humbling to see how a small gesture made a face light up! It was like magic—when I called congregants by their first names, they were delighted, and some of them asked my name too. Thus, we were no longer strangers to each other but a family. As Stephen S. Wilbricht, csc, states, "All that we do in liturgy is about discovering ever deeper the bonds of unity that we share in Christ" (page 60).

> It was humbling to see how a small gesture made a face light up! It was like magic—when I called congregants by their first names, they were delighted, and some of them asked my name too.

Pastor

Father Patrick A. Smith

People from many nations have heard the voices of the extraordinary gospel choir at my parish, St. Augustine Catholic Church. Whether singing at the Vatican for papal audiences or performing at concerts in France, Germany, Mexico, or the White House, the choir has been a powerful megaphone singing God's praises and announcing the good news. For many special occasions throughout the year, the choir performs in concerts at the parish. As much as I love those concerts, I am most edified when the choir ministers in the context of the Sunday liturgy.

In relationship to our choir, one of my proudest moments as pastor was the day that the choir celebrated the anniversary of their founding and, teaming up with our homeless outreach ministry, performed in a concert at a park in downtown Washington, DC, where dozens of homeless people sleep daily. What a wonderful way, I thought, "to make our assemblies places where justice is realized" (page 59). What a practical and effective way to "visibly connect our worship to our baptismal obligation to work for God's just kingdom" (page 59).

I was especially heartened by this event because the leaders of our homeless outreach ministry and that of the gospel choir had come up with this idea on their own. It was a powerful affirmation that my years of teaching and preaching about the connection between liturgy and life, worship and service, giving thanks to God and doing justice to God's people had an effect on parishioners. The concert in the park, where free food and supplies were distributed, was planned and executed by lay men and women who had successfully recaptured the communal nature of the sacramental grace conferred on them in baptism. There we were on a Sunday afternoon in a public park, living tabernacles, dwelling places for God, proclaiming the Gospel in song, in word, and in deed.

❖ Discussion Questions ❖

1. How does the parish staff encourage the faithful to understand that they are participating in the Mass as a body united to others?

2. Do we recognize that, along with our responsibilities in our designated ministry, we need to be attentive to building up our community into a dwelling place of God?

3. How does even a small gesture such as learning and using a person's name build community?

4. Do we encourage our parishioners to go out into the community to build up the dwelling place of God?

5. How can our assembly be formed to be a place where justice is realized?

Prayer

Hymn Suggestion

✳ "Where Charity and Love Prevail," World Library Publications, Inc., 1962.

Reading   (Mark 3:31–35)

His [Jesus'] mother and his brothers arrived. Standing outside they sent word to him and called him. A crowd seated around him told him, "Your mother and your brothers [and your sisters] are outside asking for you." But he said to them in reply, "Who are my mother and [my] brothers?" And looking around at those seated in the circle he said, "Here are my mother and my brothers. For whoever does the will of God is my brother and sister and mother."

> ### ❧ Reflection ❧
>
> Participation in the Lord's Supper, in the regular Eucharistic celebration of the Church, entails the ongoing reordering of relationships. In fact, sacramental celebration in general is always a re-membering of Christ in his Body. In a very real sense, Jesus manifests this sacramental principle in this scene in which he names his disciples as his brothers and sisters. His relationships with his family are no less important to him now than in the past; however, these relationships have been reordered because of the demands of the mission. The mission creates new bonds of fidelity and commitment. Participation in the Eucharist and the other sacraments reminds us that our relationships must always be renewed according to our oneness in Christ.

Prayer of the Faithful

To our Lord, who has made us his sons and daughters, we pray:

✳ For the Church in her mission of maintaining and manifesting the Body of Christ, we pray: **Gracious Lord, hear our prayer.**

✳ For the world, especially for war-torn countries and those nations ravaged by extreme poverty, we pray: **Gracious Lord, hear our prayer.**

✳ For broken relationships, especially for married couples seeking a divorce, we pray: **Gracious Lord, hear our prayer.**

✳ For new relationships, especially for couples seeking the sacrament of marriage, we pray:
Gracious Lord, hear our prayer.

✳ For families, especially for brother and sisters who harbor resentment against each other, we pray:
Gracious Lord, hear our prayer.

✳ For the dead who have gone before us and await the day of redemption, we pray:
Gracious Lord, hear our prayer.

Gathering these petitions, let us pray as the Lord taught us:

Our Father . . .

Collect

Lord Jesus Christ,

you call us your brothers and sisters

whenever we strive to do the Father's will

and live in your love.

May your Church truly be your living Body on earth

and reveal to all the hope of an eternal

dwelling place in the world to come.

For you live and reign with the Father

in the unity of the Holy Spirit, God, for ever and ever.

Amen.

CHAPTER 6

Adopted Sons and Daughters

For those who are led by the Spirit of God are children of God. For you did not receive a spirit of slavery to fall back into fear, but you received a spirit of adoption, through which we cry, "Abba, Father!"

—Romans 8:14–15

The primeval account of the world's foundation described in the Book of Genesis reveals that all of creation is called "good" by God (see Genesis 1). Every living plant, every drop of rain, every creature under heaven comes from the loving design of God and is meant to radiate beauty and praise back to the Creator. At the same time, Christians believe that baptism provides the human creation with the dignity of a new relationship of being called adopted sons and daughters of God. The general introduction to *Christian Initiation* states: "For, having been incorporated into Christ through Baptism, they are formed into the People of God, and having received the remission of all their sins and been rescued from the power of darkness, they are brought to the status of adopted sons and daughters, being made a new creation by water and the Holy Spirit. Hence they are called, and indeed are, children of God." [1] The word *status*, in this description of baptism, denotes not privilege but responsibility. Grafted onto Christ, Christians are necessarily responsible for the mission he left behind. "Go, therefore, and make disciples of all nations" (Matthew 28:19).

---

1. CI, 2.

The designation of Christians as adopted children of God is intrinsic to the work of social justice. Take, for example, the Catholic social teaching on the theme of solidarity. In its simplest form, solidarity is the work of recognizing that we are all part of one family. Race, nationality, gender, age, wealth do not bring about distinctions; instead, all members of the human family are meant to be able to participate fully. It is even possible to say that solidarity demands the inclusion of a healthy relationship with natural resources and every fiber of creation. Pope Francis writes in *The Joy of the Gospel*:

> The word *solidarity* is a little worn and at times poorly understood, but it refers to something more than a few sporadic acts of generosity. It presumes the creation of a new mindset which thinks in terms of community and the priority of the life of all over the appropriation of goods by a few.[2]

The change in mindset to which Pope Francis refers concerns recognizing interdependence. Thus, being called an adopted son or daughter of God in no way is meant to call the Christian away from the world; instead, it necessarily demands a commitment to the common good. Baptism is not an escape from the world, but a deeper immersion into the pursuit of caring for all aspects of creation. In the words of Pope John Paull II in his encyclical *On Social Concern* (*Sollicitudo rei socialis*), "It is above all a question of interdependence, sensed as a system determining relationships in the contemporary world, in its economic, cultural, political and religious elements, and accepted as a moral category. When interdependence becomes recognized in this way, the correlative response as a moral and social attitude, as a 'virtue,' is solidarity."[3]

Another way of talking about solidarity is to say that sacrifice must be an important part of the Christian vocation. Sacrifice is a foundational facet of the paschal mystery, as we believe that Jesus chose the way of

---

2. EG, 188.

3. John Paul II, *Sollicitudo rei socialis* (December 30, 1987), 38.

self-sacrifice over the way of self-preservation as gift bestowed to the Father. Sacrifice is furthermore based upon the fundamental right of human dignity—namely, that any form of poverty or oppression ought to be an offense to the children of God. Just as the Acts of the Apostles portrays members of the early Church working to alleviate the needs of the poor (see Acts 2:44–45), so are Christians today meant to sacrifice to end poverty and hunger. This means not simply providing a stopgap through charitable giving, but by demonstrating in action that Christianity cannot allow people to slip through the cracks. Baptism demands that we work for a oneness in creation that is rooted in divine love. "In a world marked by extreme discrepancies between the rich and the poor," writes Bernard Evans, "the practice of solidarity necessarily calls for sacrifice."[4]

Recognizing the bonds of baptism that unite all the adopted children of God is also intimately connected to the Church's teaching on the dignity of work and workers' rights. When God completed the work of creation, he designated a day for rest, as this becomes the opportunity for all to take the time to contemplate the grandeur of creation as well as the abundant love of the Creator. Work is thus meant to be a sign of personal creativity as well as the accomplishment of an act of love for others. Rather than viewing work as drudgery and oppressive to the human spirit, the Church views work as a gift from God bestowed upon creation, so that we might be collaborators in perfecting his cosmic creation. *Gaudium et spes* states, "When they (human beings) work, not only do they transform matter and society, they also perfect themselves. They learn, develop their faculties, emerging from and transcending themselves. Rightly understood, this kind of growth is more precious than any kind of wealth."[5]

---

4. Bernard Evans, *Glorifying the Lord by Your Life: Catholic Social Teaching and the Liturgy* (Chicago: Liturgy Training Publications, 2020), 60.

5. GS, 35.

Unfortunately, many people do not experience their work as fulfilling or transformative. For many people, labor is just a means of providing a paycheck that will be used to support a family and to pay the bills. Rather than being self-expressive and creative, work can be alienating and life-draining. This is where parish leadership could generate possibilities for work on behalf of the Christian community that would allow for a creative expenditure of energy. Recognizing that we are all adopted children of God should awaken our hearts to labor for those who struggle to survive in our wider community. Gathering as brothers and sisters to repair the roof of a neighborhood widow, organizing a food drive, and tutoring in an aftercare program are examples of simple ways in which the positive nature of work is experienced.

Furthermore, our common baptism in the Lord demands that we must advocate for men and women who are underemployed and assist the unemployed to find meaningful labor. This is something that the gathered assembly should be regularly praying for in its intercessory prayer on Sunday, but it also demands a commitment to enact change within our society. In its pastoral letter on economic justice, the United States Conference of Catholic Bishops (USCCB) defines the importance of quality work as follows:

> All work has a threefold moral significance. First, it is a principal way that people exercise the distinctive human capacity for self-expression and self-realization. Second, it is the ordinary way for human beings to fulfill their material needs. Finally, work enables people to contribute to the well-being of the larger community. Work is not only for oneself. It is for one's family, for the nation, and indeed for the benefit of the entire human family.[6]

---

6. United States Catholic Bishops, *Economic Justice for All: Pastoral Letter on Catholic Social Teaching and the U.S. Economy* (Washington, DC: National Conference of Catholic Bishop, 1986), 97.

Access to quality work provides one with the opportunity for greater participation within society and therefore the greater likelihood to be incorporated in a web of relationship. The USCCB goes on to suggest that "freedom, initiative, and creativity" (100), which are all constituents of meaningful labor, are necessary in building up a healthy community. "The task of creating a more just US economy is the vocation of all and depends on strengthening the virtues of public service and responsible citizenship in personal life and on all levels of institutional life."[7]

The moral imperatives of solidarity (or interdependence) with the human community as well as all of creation and the dignity of workers and labor in general are two aspects of Catholic social teaching that are intrinsically connected to our baptism. Because the waters of baptism incorporate us into one Body of God's adopted sons and daughters, no one ought to escape our personal concern and care. All have a responsibility to act with justice for those not only within the local parish community or civic community, but also for those who live in foreign lands thousands of miles away. Parish leadership has the responsibility to try to open the eyes of all believers to the realities of suffering and injustice that exist on our planet. This is yet another way in which Christian baptism is a discipleship of pilgrimage; ours is not a vocation of being rooted in place but rather of being uprooted for the sake of the Gospel.

Parish leadership has the responsibility to try to open the eyes of all believers to the realities of suffering and injustice that exist on our planet.

7. *Economic Justice for All*, 100.

❧ Pastoral Reflections ❧

Religious Educator

Cristina Castillo

Baptism unites us into the Body of Christ. Together we are called to be alert and create change. We are also called to create opportunities for growth, whether personal or spiritual. Whether paid or volunteer, any kind of work allows people to feel accomplished, and in the environment of our parish communities, workers and volunteers contribute to the local and universal Church. We are allowed to foster the relationship of God with children, youth, and anyone else who belongs to the parish. Ministry leaders can notice and discover the gifts and talents of those in their care.

Sonia was a parish office assistant while studying for a master's degree in theology. Even with her graduation approaching, she felt she was not qualified to apply for a position as formation coordinator. I could see in Sonia a wealth of knowledge, gifts, talents, and a passion for formation. Once Sonia graduated, I approached her with the application for a diocesan coordinating position. She was reluctant to apply but after much encouragement she sent her resume and a month later she began her new job.

Let us look at Carolina: a former confirmation student, she is now a high school senior looking for her first job. At such a young age she had already developed an excellent work ethic. During her time in the confirmation program, she would arrive early to help the catechists set up their classrooms and would also assist with the first Communion student dismissals. I extended an invitation to an internship to Carolina, and when she left

When opportunities are extended, we assist people in becoming accountable to themselves and their local parish community.

for college, she was hired to work in an office, a job that helped her pay her tuition. Carolina minored in religious studies for her undergraduate degree and is now pursuing a master's degree in pastoral studies. When opportunities are extended, we assist people in becoming accountable to themselves and their local parish community. We also open doors to possibilities that may have not been considered.

Music Minister

Michael Conrady

Aware of a lack of American Sign Language (ASL) resources in our area of the diocese, our parish established a deaf ministry. A Sunday Mass time was determined for the signing of the liturgy, an ASL interpreter was found, and word was spread about the new parish ministry.

To offer the deaf community a place to gather that did not draw attention from the ritual action, seats were reserved at the edge of the assembly and a small lectern was set up for the interpreter in the corner of the church. Each Sunday, the number of deaf people worshiping with us grew. Formation was offered after Mass, and the parish became accustomed to seeing this small but faithful flock at church.

The story could have ended there. But in conversation with members of the deaf community, we learned that our model had missed the mark. In our zeal to help deaf people participate at Mass, we created a situation that hampered it. These children of God were roped off, separated from the main assembly, and offered an interpreter in a corner for their focus. We had, effectively, created second-class Christians in our midst and built barriers that prevented them from experiencing Christ in the liturgy.

Upon our request for suggestions to improve worship, the deaf community recommended that they be seated in a centrally located area and that the ASL interpreter shadow the priest and other ministers so that the liturgical action could be followed as it occurred. Additionally, our priests learned ASL phrases so they could both speak and sign the dialogues with the assembly. Cantors and lectors learned basic phrases, and the assembly responded enthusiastically by signing phrases and words such as AMEN and THANKS BE TO GOD, even as they said the words. I will never forget the first Sunday I witnessed an entire community singing and raising its arms as its members signed an exuberant Easter ALLELUIA!

Eventually, a number of deaf people answered the call to serve as liturgical ministers. Ushers, sacristans, ministers of hospitality, and even readers were trained and formed. In the week before Mass, a deaf reader would study the Scriptures, work out elegant and faithful translations in ASL, and meet with clergy to practice proclaiming the Word. On Sundays, the reader would proclaim the Word at the ambo while an English interpreter stood to their side and read the Scriptures for people who were not deaf. These readers had a powerful impact on the assembly and also symbolized an integrated community living out the gifts of their baptism.

While it is gratifying to reflect on a marginalized community being welcomed at the table, the entire parish community was transformed. By honoring the baptism of every person and working together to include all who had been marginalized, our entire community was changed, and in a foretaste of that great heavenly banquet, we truly became the Body of Christ for one another.

Volunteer Coordinator   Caroline Okello

> Rather than viewing work as drudgery and oppressive to the human spirit, the Church views work as a gift from God bestowed upon creation, so that we might be collaborators in perfecting his cosmic creation. (page 69)

For me, work is not just about pay but service to others. I was delighted to obtain a position in direct service work to immigrants and refugees who had journeyed to the United States as I did. I enjoyed my work, I worked hard, and my supervisor seemed to appreciate my work. But after three years his attitude toward me changed, and the work environment became hostile toward me, with even some of my peers treating me differently.

Talking to my boss did not change matters and neither did speaking to his supervisor or to the human resources director, both of whom were friends with my boss. Feeling helpless, I sensed the reality of systemic racism: it was three white males in leadership against one non-white immigrant woman. The work that I had so enjoyed had become a nightmare.

With no one to support me, I needed to advocate for myself. This was especially important since I support my aging mother and physically disabled brother. When I send them money, it ripples in the community through the groceries they purchase, and the rent and other bills they pay in the local community. In this way, my pay sustains a whole village. As the Catholic bishops of the United States state in *Economic Justice for All*, "Work is not only for oneself. It is for one's family, for the nation, and indeed for the benefit of the entire human family" (*Economic Justice for All*, 97).

While I was fighting for my job, God had other plans! As stated in Isaiah 14:24: "The LORD of hosts has sworn: / 'As I have resolved, / so shall it be; / As I have planned, so shall it stand.'" I was blessed with a new position.

While I didn't win my battle for fair treatment in my previous job, I received something more important: the realization that God was fighting for me! Just when my hope was almost lost, I was offered a new position in the parish I love. The work has been life-giving, a wonderful opportunity for me to grow and discover talents.

Pastor

Father Patrick A. Smith

"Do you know the date of your baptism?" I asked parents and godparents attending the catechetical session that occurs prior to infant baptisms. Embarrassed smiles and silence were the response. When I questioned this lack of knowledge, a brave soul responded, "Father, I was rather young at the time." Others humorously agreed. I then queried, "What is your date of birth?" All knew their birth date and acknowledged that it occurred before their baptism.

In the Disney movie *The Lion King*, the main character has a vision of his deceased father telling him, "Simba, you have forgotten me."

"No, father, I could never forget you," Simba replies.

"You have forgotten me because you have forgotten who you are," the father says. "You are my son. . . . Remember who you are!"

When I queried the parents and godparents, I was interested in knowing whether they know who they are. God calls us to *be* before God calls us to *do*. In the evangelist John's first letter, he notes our status as children of God: "See what love the Father has bestowed on us that we may be called the children of God. Yet so we are" (1 John 3:1). How could we possibly know that we are God's adopted sons and daughters if no one ever celebrates it, acknowledges it, or reminds us of its significance and the duties that are part of it? How could we ever realize that, precisely because of our baptism, we "all have a responsibility to act with justice for those not only within the local parish community or civic community, but also for those who live in foreign lands thousands of miles away" (page 71)? How could "the eyes of all believers"

> How could we possibly know that we are God's adopted sons and daughters if no one ever celebrates it; acknowledges it; or reminds us of its significance and the duties that are part of it?

be open to and respond to "the realities of suffering and injustice that exist on our planet" if they can't see the love the Father has bestowed on them—if they don't remember who they are?

❖ Discussion Questions ❖

1. When have you acted in solidarity with another by pointing out a path toward fulfilling work that uses their strengths and talents?

2. How can your parish community collaborate with others and make a commitment to work for the common good?

3. What can the parish do to stand with people whose livelihood has been threatened by prejudice and discrimination?

4. How can the parish improve the ways it catechizes and forms parishioners so that they realize that they are children of God and have a duty to act with justice?

5. How does the parish seek to open parishioners' eyes to realities of suffering and injustice?

PRAYER

Hymn Suggestion

"Abba! Father!" Rory Cooney, OCP Publications, Inc., 1977.

Reading   (Mark 1:7–11)

This is what he [John the Baptist] proclaimed: "One mightier than I is coming after me. I am not worthy to stoop and loosen the thongs of his sandals. I have baptized you with water; he will baptize you with the holy Spirit."

It happened in those days that Jesus came from Nazareth of Galilee and was baptized in the Jordan by John. On coming up out of the water he saw the heavens being torn open and the Spirit, like a dove, descending upon him. And a voice came from the heavens, "You are my beloved Son; with you I am well pleased."

> ### ❧ Reflection ❧
>
> Theological minds have argued over the centuries over this question: Did Jesus really need to be baptized? Some would argue that his baptism was merely pro forma and that he allowed himself to be baptized by his cousin, John, only to ally himself with the kingdom. Others would argue that a new identity was bestowed upon Jesus in the waters of the Jordan and that he suddenly became convinced of his intimate union with the Father, who made clear that he was "well pleased" with all that Jesus had done up to that point. Regardless, the point is that the surrender of self and professing allegiance to the work of the kingdom bestows an indelible mark. Just as the Spirit seals the identity of Jesus at his baptism, so are all who are baptized into him made beloved daughters and sons of God. God knows us from the moment we begin to take shape in our mother's womb, but baptism into Christ allows us a share in a filial relationship, a relationship that is meant to unfold in the arduous work of announcing the coming of the kingdom.

Prayer of the Faithful

Grateful that God has made us his sons and daughters, we pray:

* For those preparing for baptism, that they may fully discover their vocation as priest, prophet, and king, we pray:
  Lord, hear our prayer.

* For all who experience war, that they may know peace, we pray:
  Lord, hear our prayer.

* For those who have rejected their baptismal commitment, that they may recognize again their true identity as adopted children of God, we pray: **Lord, hear our prayer.**

✳ For all the unemployed and underemployed and for those who are imprisoned in slavery, that they may find fulfilling work, we pray:
Lord, hear our prayer.

✳ For all who experience pain and illness in their bodies and who sometimes know great isolation, that they may be surrounded by the support of the Body of Christ, we pray:
Lord, hear our prayer.

Gathering these petitions, let us pray as the Lord taught us:

Our Father . . .

Collect

> Abba, Father,
> in the waters of the River Jordan,
> you made known your beloved Son.
> In these same waters,
> we are reborn
> as your adopted sons and daughters.
> May we learn to renew our baptism daily,
> so as to serve you in the image and likeness of your Son,
> our Lord Jesus Christ,
> who lives and reigns with you in the unity of the Holy Spirit,
> God, for ever and ever.
> Amen.

CHAPTER 7

A Royal Priesthood,
a Holy Nation

You are "a chosen race, a royal priesthood, a holy nation, a people
of his own, so that you may announce the praises" of him who
called you out of darkness into his wonderful light.

—1 Peter 2:9

E xodus 19 contains a beautiful description of the Israelites, who have
recently been set free from slavery in Egypt. God calls Moses to
prepare himself and the people for the reception of the covenant. The
encounter unfolds as follows:

> Moses went up to the mountain of God. Then the LORD called to
> him from the mountain, saying: This is what you will say to the
> house of Jacob; tell the Israelites: You have seen how I treated the
> Egyptians and how I bore you up on eagles' wings and brought you
> to myself. Now, if you obey me completely and keep my covenant,
> you will be my treasured possession among all peoples, though all
> the earth is mine. You will be to me a kingdom of priests, a holy
> nation. That is what you must tell the Israelites. So, Moses went and
> summoned the elders of the people. When he set before them all that
> the LORD had ordered him to tell them, all the people answered
> together, "Everything the LORD has said, we will do." Then Moses
> brought back to the LORD the response of the people. (Exodus 19:3–8)

In the Book of Exodus, priestly identity as well as consecrated status depend upon keeping the covenant. Holding fast to the covenant marks the people as chosen by God. When Israel leaves Mount Sinai and begins its forty-year journey throughout the wilderness en route to the Promised Land, Israel would also have to offer burnt sacrifices to God to visibly manifest its fidelity. The selection of choice animals to be sacrificed by the priests of the tabernacle gave witness to the people's ongoing trust in God's guidance and protection of them.

The levitical priesthood involved a ritual dedication, whereby those born into the priestly line of Aaron were set apart to offer sacrifices on behalf of the people.[1] Priests were adorned in elaborate vestments, worn so that they could be identified for the role they played in the community, a role that demanded the maintenance of purity. Thus, holiness came to mean the ability to avoid defilement. It was not so much that these chosen men had a deeper relationship with God but that they were committed to standing before God in a state of ritual purity.

Lumen gentium employs the image of a priestly people early in the document, describing the Church as a sacred assembly far before it considers ecclesial hierarchy. *Lumen gentium* describes the priesthood of the faithful as follows:

> Christ the Lord, high priest taken from the midst of humanity (see Hebrews 5:1–5), made the new people "a kingdom of priests to his God and Father" (Apocalypse 1:6; see 5:9–10). The baptized, by regeneration and the anointing of the holy Spirit, are consecrated as a spiritual house and a holy priesthood, that through all their Christian activities they may offer spiritual sacrifices and proclaim the marvels of him who has called them out of darkness into his wonderful light (see 1 Peter 2:4–10). Therefore, all the disciples of Christ, persevering in prayer and praising God (see Acts 2:42–27), should present themselves as a sacrifice, living, holy and pleasing to

---

1. See Exodus 29.

God (see Romans 12:1). They should everywhere on earth bear witness to Christ and give an answer to everyone who asks a reason for their hope of eternal life (see 1 Peter 3:15). [2]

Two important distinctions need to be made between the priesthood of the faithful and the ancient pattern and practice of the priesthood of the old covenant. First, instead of sacrificing animals, disciples of Christ are called to offer their entire lives as a sacrifice to God. The priestly duty of offering up to God continues to apply to all the baptized; their offering is not cattle and sheep, but a humble and contrite heart. [3] Second, unlike the Levites of the Israelite community, who needed to maintain a distance from the ordinary lives of the members of the tribe to preserve their holiness, *Lumen gentium* declares that the priesthood of the faithful is to testify to Christ "everywhere on earth." The call to holiness is not an invitation to dwell apart from others but rather to radiate Christ's presence in every part of the world. Mary A. Ehle outlines the diverse ways in which Christians respond to the call to holiness by enacting their role as a priestly people:

> The call to holiness is not an invitation to dwell apart from others but rather to radiate Christ's presence in every part of the world.

> Daily we live as priestly people when we reflect on how we make present the holiness and sacredness that is inside of us and then act accordingly. When we honor the holiness and sacredness in every man, woman, and child we encounter by speaking words that build others up rather than tear them down, we acknowledge the holiness within all God's people. When we lead prayer in our communities, in small groups, in our homes, and among our friends we embody our identity as members of God's priestly people. We do this when we offer ourselves and the gifts of bread and wine to become the

2. LG, 10.

3. See Psalm 51.

Body and Blood of Christ at Mass. When we pray for the needs of others and for their salvation. And, when our prayer invites and welcomes the stranger, the immigrant, the homeless, and the brokenhearted to participate, we recognize how our holiness merges with theirs and together we can seek new ways of loving one another and affirming the holiness inside of us.[4]

When newly baptized infants emerge from the waters of the font, they are anointed with the sacred chrism on the forehead with the accompanying prayer: "Almighty God, the Father of our Lord Jesus Christ, / has freed you from sin, / given you new birth by water and the Holy Spirit, / and joined you to his people. / He now anoints you with the Chrism of salvation, / so that you may remain members of Christ, Priest, Prophet and King, / unto eternal life."[5] This prayer of anointing—not to be confused with confirmation—highlights what has been accomplished in baptism (that is, freedom from sin, new birth, and incorporation into the Church) and also outlines the future vocation of the newly made disciple to be carried all the way into heaven (that is, "remain members of Christ, Priest, Prophet and King"). We are not called to be the priest, nor the prophet, nor the king; instead, we are called to "remain" in him and to discover daily what these three titles of Christ are all about.

All three titles are representative of the servant-nature of Christ, the one who came not to be served but to serve (see Mark 10:45, Matthew 20:28). As previously discussed, participation in the priesthood of Christ calls us to pattern our life after Christ's and to present it as a spiritual sacrifice to the Father. What about the titles of prophet and king? It might be tempting to say that these roles, like that of priest, belong to the institutional hierarchy of the Church. However, all Christians participate in Christ's servant leadership.

---

4. Ehle, *Anointed for Discipleship: The Meaning of Baptism for Our Christian Life*, 14.
5. *Order of Baptism of Children* (OBC), 62.

Perhaps at this point in the history of the world, when people of so many diverse perspectives on life are linked in a global network of relationships, more than ever, the importance of lay leadership in the Church needs to be identified. The Church needs to make a difference in a secular society that is quickly losing sight of the divine. Baptism demands that Christian disciples bring the light of Christ into the darkened world. *Lumen gentium* states:

> To be secular is the special characteristic of the laity. . . . It is the special vocation of the laity to seek the kingdom of God by engaging in temporal affairs and directing them according to God's will. They live in the world, in each and every one of the world's occupations and callings and in the ordinary circumstances of social and family life which, as it were, form the context of their existence. There they are called by God to contribute to the sanctification of the world from within, like leaven, in the spirit to the Gospel, by fulfilling their own particular duties. Thus, especially by the witness of their life, resplendent in faith, hope and charity they manifest Christ to others. It is their special task to illuminate and order all temporal matters in which they are closely involved in such a way that these are always carried out and develop in Christ's way and to the praise of the Creator and Redeemer.[6]

Lay men and women perform the prophetic function of Christ when they strive to proclaim the truth of the Gospel "in temporal affairs," thereby "directing them according to God's will." In other words, all the baptized are commissioned, by word and by action, to bring the good news of Christ into the workplace, the school, the playground—in short, the entire world in which they are immersed. Similarly, baptismal leadership is exercised when disciples strive to manifest the kingly office of Christ which is accomplished by enacting the paschal mystery, choosing the way of death to selfishness and ego so that life may be lived for others.

---

6. LG, 31.

Being anointed with chrism so as to "remain members of Christ"—who is priest, prophet, and king—commissions all the baptized to a way of servant discipleship. Christians are to learn daily that the suffering of the cross brings the resurrection of Easter. The way of holiness is learned not only by weekly participation in the Eucharist but in the challenge to live as the selfless King in our ordinary lives.

❧ Pastoral Reflections ❧

Religious Educator
Cristina Castillo

Living out our baptismal call requires that we become beacons of hope while remaining true to the covenant made on our behalf during baptism. Psalm 51 offers an outline of how we should live. Parish leaders must live as role models, embodying what it means to be disciples of Christ.

A few years ago, during one of our formation Saturdays, I ran into a young woman who was hurting and desperately seeking help. In that moment, all she needed was someone to listen and let her know she was created in the image of God. She did not need to be judged or be told what to do. Embodying Christ for the dear neighbor may mean offering someone a ride, giving food to the hungry, picking up groceries for an elderly neighbor, or listening to a life story. There is no one way to be Christ for the neighbor; the possibilities are endless.

As human beings, all of us have flaws, but we must strive to live as holy people and portray Christ on earth. It is essential that we live what we teach. The catechist who just taught his students about the parable of the good Samaritan is called on to serve the homeless man that he encounters as he leaves the parish. It is his duty, for example, to ask if the man needs food or water. The catechist who ignores or scorns the man would not be living out the teaching just given to the students. Our actions speak volumes. If we only teach the lessons but not live by example, we become unfaithful witnesses. As baptized people, we have a duty to a greater mission: to bring the good news to others by evangelizing with words and with our actions.

Music Minister

Michael Conrady

Priest. Prophet. King. It is fair to say that most Catholics probably do not reflect on their participation of this threefold ministry of Christ, despite the dedication prayers that took place at their baptism. Yet this ministry is expressed in ways that are felt in the community and experienced in the Church.

I benefited from growing up in a parish with ordained and lay leaders who took seriously the Second Vatican Council exhortation to foster the priesthood of the faithful. When I began to show signs of musical talent at a young age, I was encouraged to use my gifts in the community. Even before my confirmation, I was active in the liturgical and musical life of my parish. By the time I was in high school, I was leading a choir and playing the organ.

> These parish leaders guided and formed me so that, as *Lumen gentium* states, I would serve others to the glory of God, and in so doing, remain in Christ.

Looking back, I see how a lifetime of ministry was born from parish leaders who took seriously the call to holiness in *Lumen gentium* and encouraged my lay vocation at a young age. These parish leaders guided and formed me so that, as *Lumen gentium* states, I would serve others to the glory of God, and in so doing, remain in Christ.

As a lay minister, my modeling of these priestly gifts and talents in the community is particularly visible: I help facilitate the prayer of the community through sung prayer. I assist with the celebration of the sacraments. I provide music for baptisms, weddings, and funerals. I train and empower other members of the community. It is no small responsibility to know that in sharing the good news, comforting the afflicted, and proclaiming justice for the oppressed, I am also participating in an essential and ancient tradition of prophecy that dates back to the Hebrew Scriptures. These gifts are real and visible manifestations of my baptismal dedication as well as the priesthood of the faithful in the Body of Christ.

Volunteer Coordinator

Caroline Okello

What does it mean, as a layperson, to "remain members of Christ, Priest, Prophet and King"? At first, those words may not seem to be part of our lives. It's easy to hear those words and think they don't have anything to do with me. But when we witness to the work of God in our lives, we find ourselves manifesting Christ to the world, even when we least expect it.

Several years ago, during the Christmas Vigil Mass, prompted by the Holy Spirit, I noticed a flier for a program offering free support for preparation to become a citizen. Since I was eligible for citizenship, I made the call and became enrolled in the sessions. About six months later, I was a naturalized citizen of the United States of America. Soon afterward, I was hired as a community acti-vation coordinator, with responsibility to recruit, orient, and train volunteers who would support immigrants and refugees in different capacities.

> When we witness to the work of God in our lives, we find ourselves manifesting Christ to the world, even when we least expect it.

A year after I was in this position, my pastor asked me to speak about my work at all five Masses. The experience was nerve-wracking. Never had I imagined that I would stand before over a thousand congregants at each Mass to describe my immigration journey. On the other hand, I was pleased to share my testimony of God's love and mercy. I depended entirely on God as I spoke, identifying with the words of Psalm 23:4: "Even though I walk through the valley of the shadow of death, / I will fear no evil, for you are with me; / your rod and your staff comfort me."

Before long, I agreed to be a witness in parishes in the archdiocese, explaining the needs of immigrants and refugees and how parishioners and the community can support them. I told my story of my journey to the United States, why I needed to come, the obstacles and challenges I encountered, and who supported me when I settled in the country.

As I let others hear my story, over and over, listeners have become motivated to support immigrants and refugees in various ways, including teaching English for speakers of other languages, accompaniment, inter-preting and translating, and teaching basic computer skills. Meanwhile, I became more confident with public speaking. One year, I volunteered to be the emcee at the annual Catholic immigration summit in the archdio-cese, and now each Sunday, I serve as a reader at Mass. Still anxious about standing in front of a congregation, I rely on God and say a quick prayer to the Holy Spirit before I proclaim the Scripture.

Pastor Father Patrick A. Smith

While celebrating a nuptial Mass recently, I was reminded of words from a sermon by an unknown author, for the sacrament of matrimony. "Sacrifice is usually difficult and irksome. Only love can make it easy and perfect love can make it a joy," the sermon reads in part. I love this quote yet too often I forget its central message that sacrifice can be a joy!

The young couple both had been active in parish ministry prior to their engagement. As I witnessed the bride and groom look into each other's eyes during their wedding vows, I knew that they understood that love and sacrifice are two sides of the same coin. This couple consciously lived out their priestly identity as disciples of Jesus; the identity they received on the day they were baptized into the priestly, prophetic, and kingly ministry of Christ. In fact, they had fallen in love with Christ before they fell in love with each other.

In my homily, I reminded the soon-to-be married couple that at the end of every wedding, the bride and groom are the first to walk down the aisle and out of the church. In that moment, I explained to them, they embody not only the great commandment "Love one another as I have loved you" (John 13:34), but the great commission: "Go, therefore, and make disciples of all nations, baptizing them in the name of the Father, and of the Son, and of the holy Spirit, teaching them to observe all that I have commanded you" (Matthew 28:19–20). The married couple are called to be heralds of the good news.

In a world that has grown cynical about the possibility of lasting love, the married couple lives their vocation daily, giving prophetic witness to all who have eyes to see that true love keeps its promises. I hope that my ordained ministry as priest has served and inspired this couple. Their royal priesthood has inspired and reminded me of something I too easily forget: that love too can make sacrifice easy and perfect love can make it a joy.

❂ Discussion Questions ❂

1. How do you offer yourself to others to accompany them in times of pain and need?

2. In what ways can the parish help its members to fulfill their call to act as priest, prophet, and king by pointing out and nourishing gifts?

3. Can the parish improve how it encourages the faithful to act as priest, prophet, and king in the ways that they use their gifts in the community?

4. When do you tie evangelization into your teaching and preaching on the sacraments, helping your parishioners understand that the sacraments call us to be heralds of the good news?

5. In your teaching, your homilies, or your attitude, how do you portray that the call to holiness is a call to radiate Christ in our daily interactions?

Prayer

Hymn Suggestion

✳ "God Has Chosen Me," Bernadette Farrell, OCP Publications, 1990.

✳ "Out of Darkness," Christopher Walker, OCP Publications, 1989.

Reading (Romans 1:1–7)

Paul, a slave of Christ Jesus, called to be an apostle and set apart for the gospel of God, which he promised previously through his prophets in the holy scriptures, the gospel about his Son, descended from David according to the flesh, but established as Son of God in power according to the Spirit of holiness through resurrection from the dead, Jesus Christ our Lord. Through him we have received the grace of apostleship, to bring about the obedience of faith, for the sake of his name, among all the Gentiles, among whom are you also, who are called to belong to Jesus Christ; to all the beloved of God in Rome, called to be holy. Grace to you and peace from God our Father and the Lord Jesus Christ.

> ### ❧ Reflection ❧
>
> Paul's exhortation to the Church of Rome as Christians "called to be holy" is echoed in the Second Vatican Council's *Lumen gentium*, which states: "It is therefore quite clear that all Christians in any state or walk of life are called to the fullness of the Christian life and to the perfection of charity, and this holiness is conducive to a more human way of living even in society here on earth. In order to reach this perfection, the faithful should use the strength dealt out to them by Christ's gift, so that, following in his footsteps and conformed to his image, doing the will of God in everything, they may wholeheartedly devote themselves to the glory of God and to the service of their neighbor" (40). Just as Paul told the Romans that, like him, they "have received the grace of apostleship," so too are all of us meant to witness to the Lord's resurrection in every aspect of our daily living.

Prayer of the Faithful

To our Lord, who calls us to holiness, we pray:

* For Christian women and men, that they may grow in holiness and in Christ's image for the good of our world, we pray:
Gracious Lord, hear our prayer.

* For all who live unconcerned with the struggles of others, that they may experience a conversion of heart, we pray:
Gracious Lord, hear our prayer.

* For the sick and those who manifest the paschal mystery of Christ in their daily suffering, we pray:
Gracious Lord, hear our prayer.

* For the ability to live out the priestly nature of our Christian vocation by lifting up the world to God in the sacrifice of prayer, we pray: **Gracious Lord, hear our prayer.**

* For the dead and those who care for the dying, that they may together behold the mercy of God, we pray: **Gracious Lord, hear our prayer.**

Gathering our petitions, let us pray as the Lord taught us:

Our Father . . .

Collect

Father,

giver of everything that is good,

you sent your Son into this world

to establish the way to holiness.

Baptized into the name of Jesus,

help us to grow always in his likeness.

May the obedience of faith we have received

lead to the surrender of self for the sake of Christ,

who lives and reigns with you in the unity of the Holy Spirit,

God, for ever and ever.

Amen.

CHAPTER 8

Responding to the Gospel of Christ

"But you will receive power when the holy Spirit comes upon you, and you will be my witnesses in Jerusalem, throughout Judea and Samaria, and to the ends of the earth." When he had said this, as they were looking on, he was lifted up, and a cloud took him from their sight. While they were looking intently at the sky as he was going, suddenly two men dressed in white garments stood beside them. They said, "Men of Galilee, why are you standing there looking at the sky?"

—Acts 1:8–11

The proclamation of the good news of Jesus Christ is an urgent affair placed upon the shoulders of every baptized disciple. Once one has encountered the Gospel message and has given oneself over to the project of following Jesus (a commitment made tangibly present in the sacrament of baptism), preaching the Gospel is a must. The urgency with which the Gospel must be taken out into the world is demonstrated in the opening scene in the Acts of the Apostles. Immediately prior to his ascension, the Lord charges the apostles to be his witnesses "to the ends of the earth." Instead of going right to work, they are caught gazing up at the sky. The two men question them as if to ask: "Well, what are you waiting for?"

This question must confront each baptized Christian daily: What are you waiting for? Pope John Paul II readily acknowledges the seriousness of carrying the Gospel out into the world in the 1991 encyclical *Redemptoris missio*:

> The mission *ad gentes* faces an enormous task, which in no way is disappearing. Indeed, both from the numerical standpoint of demographic increase and from the socio-cultural standpoint of the appearance of new relationships, contacts and changing situations the mission seems destined to have ever wider horizons. The task of proclaiming Jesus Christ to all peoples appears to be immense and out of all proportions to the Church's human resources. [1]

While relationships are more and more enacted on a global stage rather than localized in the context of a tight-knit community (for instance, the ability to connect virtually and so very easily with people in all corners of the globe), the requirement to make Jesus known, loved, and served has only become more indispensable. In the 1975 encyclical *Evangelii nuntiandi*, Pope Paul VI wrote of a lack of fervor in the work of Christian evangelization and the obstacles that stand in the way: "fatigue, disenchantment, compromise, lack of interest and above all lack of joy and hope." [2]

It is important to underscore, once again, that the task of evangelization belongs to every baptized Christian. Too often the clergy are considered to be experts in the field, with many parishioners believing themselves inadequately prepared for preaching the Gospel. Even when this task is explained as encompassing *how* one goes about mundane daily tasks or *how* one conducts oneself in the work setting, the vast majority of Christians continue to believe that evangelization is the work of missionaries or those who occupy the pulpit on Sundays. Even the way in which many parishes are organized betrays the universal mission

---

1. *Redemptoris missio*, 35.
2. *Evangelii nuntiandi*, 80.

to be evangelizers; just consider the way in which the *Christian initiation process* is thought to be a program that the parish sponsors rather than the very life of the parish.

In fact, let us consider for a moment the way in which the Christian initiation process apprentices catechumens in their eventual role as evangelizers. The *Rite of Christian Initiation of Adults* takes very seriously the understanding that Christian formation occurs in response to the preaching of the Gospel. One of the primary ways this formation occurs can be seen in the dismissal of the catechumens after the homily before the profession of faith and the universal prayer. Catechumens are instructed to go forth from the assembly to gather with trained catechists to listen to the Word of God once again and to apply it to their life experience. Over the course of many weeks, this breaking open of Scripture and the sharing of life within its framework impresses upon those who are maturing in the Christian faith to recognize that conversion is made in surrendering oneself to the demands of the Gospel. Their work is authentic internalization of the Word of God.

Furthermore, the RCIA envisions that regular hearing of the Word as well as well-prepared instruction on the part of catechists helps to inflame the heart of catechumens holistically, meaning they are fully prepared to live as disciples. The *Rite of Christian Initiation of Adults* states:

> The instruction that the catechumens receive during this period should be of a kind that while presenting Catholic teaching in its entirety also enlightens faith, directs the heart toward God, fosters participation in the liturgy, inspires apostolic activity, and nurtures a life completely in accord with the spirit of Christ.[3]

If one is living the lifestyle of a disciple, with heart attuned to discerning God's will and active in charity and prayer, then the Gospel is being preached. As St. Francis is credited with saying: "Preach the Gospel always, and if necessary, use words." Just as Christian formation is best

---

3. RCIA, 78.

understood as apprenticeship, whereby learning is accomplished by doing, so too is the Gospel best made known when it is witnessed rather than spoken.

Perhaps one of the most vital areas where a sound revelation of the good news needs to take place is in married life and families. There is no denying that marriage is a fragile institution in our world today. Families are also fragile, as members of the household occupy themselves with commitments outside of the home and do not make the effort to spend time together as a family. In marriage and in family life, the Gospel needs to be heard, discerned, and followed. As *Disciples Called to Witness* states: "The family, called the domestic Church, is often the first place where one experiences and is formed in the faith. . . . It is through the example of mothers and fathers, grandparents, siblings, and extended family members that one most concretely witnesses how to live a Christian life."[4]

Leading through our baptism means living the Gospel with joy. And it is not simply that I live my baptismal commitment with joy, but that the entire Body of Christ radiates a love for the world that flows from a deep penetration of the Gospel message. The baptized need to see themselves as an evangelizing community, and parish leadership would do well to help them organize for this task. In his 2013 apostolic exhortation *The Joy of the Gospel*, Pope Francis describes what it means to be an "evangelizing community":

> It is not simply that I live my baptismal commitment with joy, but that the entire Body of Christ radiates a love for the world that flows from a deep penetration of the Gospel message.

> The Church which "goes forth" is a community of missionary disciples who take the first step, who are involved and supportive, who bear fruit and rejoice. . . . Such a community has an endless desire

4. *Disciples Called to Witness*, 13.

to show mercy, the fruit of its own experience of the power of the Father's infinite mercy. . . . An evangelizing community is always concerned with fruit, because the Lord wants her to be fruitful. It cares for the grain and does not grow impatient at the weeds. The sower, when he sees weeds sprouting among the grain does not grumble or overreact. He or she finds a way to let the word take flesh in a particular situation and bear fruits of new life, however imperfect or incomplete these may appear. The disciple is ready to put his or her whole life on the line, even to accepting martyrdom, in bearing witness to Jesus Christ, yet the goal is not to make enemies but to see God's word accepted and its capacity for liberation and renewal revealed. Finally an evangelizing community is filled with joy; it knows how to rejoice always. It celebrates every small victory, every step forward in the work of evangelization.[5]

Interestingly, Pope Francis suggests that the work of evangelization on the part of all disciples is a matter of first getting involved.[6] Such is the challenge of parish administration: how to get people more involved in the life of the parish. Pastors know all too well that a small cohort of parishioners are usually the ones involved in every aspect of the parish, thereby leaving the vast majority truly unattached. Rather than simply relying on parishioners who will take on new tasks or ministries, it is better to spend time discerning gifts and talents across the board to involve all the baptized. This is working to produce an evangelizing community.

Pastoral Reflections

Religious Educator
Cristina Castillo

How do we respond to the mission Jesus began? Many people wait for others to lead and guide. What happens when a leader doesn't emerge? The

---

5. EG, 24.

6. EG, 24.

truth is we are all called to lead. We are all called to evangelize. We cannot wait for someone to appear to take the reins of our missionary responsibility. Many think that the priest, ministry leaders, or parish staff hold all the answers and that no one else could do the work. Such thinking leads to priest and minister burn out. No one new comes forward in some communities, because they know the same people will continue to help or come to the rescue.

Ministry fairs are an excellent opportunity to meet and become acquainted with parishioners. These fairs give ministries the opportunity to prepare short presentations and recruit new members. Formation programs offer parishioners the opportunity to learn more profoundly about their faith, leading to new involved lay leaders.

Many people come to their parish not knowing the many formation opportunities their parish or archdiocese or diocese has to offer. This was the case with Maria, a mother of a confirmation student. As she waited for her child to finish class, she led informal catechetical lessons with other parents. One evening, I asked if she would like to become part of the catechetical team. It took some time, but eventually Maria joined our team. I sent her to the

> Parishes need to be proactive in forming new leaders. It is essential for parish staff to be attentive to discovering parishioners' gifts and nurturing those gifts.

diocesan catechetical workshops, and she became a certified master catechist. By the time I moved on from my position, Maria had become one of the main catechetical leaders at the parish.

Parishes need to be proactive in forming new leaders. It is essential for parish staff to be attentive to discovering parishioners' gifts and nurturing those gifts. When the faithful are encouraged to attend formation sessions, they will learn more about their baptismal call and how to respond to it. When a person is formed in their faith, they will be more likely to step into a role that they previously may have found uncomfortable.

Music Minister
Michael Conrady

I was fortunate to grow up in a community where my musical gifts were encouraged and fostered. My mentors Father Bob, Sister Josephine, and

Mrs. Wood (a lay musician), encouraged me to develop my gifts and use them for the benefit of the Church. My parents sacrificed to drive me to countless lessons and endured hours of musical noise at home. Teachers, professors, and colleagues pushed me to be a better musician. Each of these people saw in me what I could not yet see, and they each invested the time and effort to help prepare me for a lifetime of service to the Gospel.

Although I could never repay this debt, there are many ways to help foster discipleship. In every parish, people at every age and stage possess gifts that are waiting to be developed and shared. Whether a young child or a seasoned lay minister, encouragement is crucial for lay vocations and ministers. Somewhere out there, a person is waiting for an affirmation or an invitation to share the good news.

Your parish may have resources to assist with this. In my parish, we have identified people with musical abilities and assisted with instrument lessons, vocal training, and other kinds of support. It is helpful to establish programs that enable parish youth to experience evangelization and ministry in a positive light. In the area of music, these programs could take the form of children's choirs, youth cantors, or even youth instrumental groups. In addition to helping young people awaken and develop their God-given gifts in an affirming environment, studies have shown that involvement in youth musical groups gives children feelings of accomplishment and well-being and sharpens important life skills.

In all of these forms of encouragement, immediate benefits may not be reaped, but seeds are being sown for a future harvest. When it comes to fostering an active, evangelizing community, we all have a role.

Volunteer Coordinator
Caroline Okello

As part of my parish ministry a few years ago, I mobilized parishioners, staff, and community members to participate in the archdiocesan pilgrimage "Walking and Witnessing for Immigrant Families." Pilgrims started the walk from the four corners of the Archdiocese of Seattle, with each group following a large cross and a banner proclaiming support for immigrant and refugee families. The journey ended with an outdoor Mass at the Northwest Detention Center, where undocumented people and asylum-seekers were detained.

During this thirteen-day journey, parishes hosted the pilgrims, providing meals and sleeping accommodations. At these stops, conversations were shared and videos were shown of the challenges facing immigrants and refugees. Along the way, we encountered many people who asked us what we were doing and where we were headed. It was wonderful to share our purpose with these strangers.

This pilgrimage was very personal for me, as I am an asylee in the United States. During the twenty-seven-mile journey to the Northwest Detention Center, I listened to immigrants' and refugees' stories of their journeys to this country, which were not that different from mine. We also prayed the Rosary, and in the spirit of diversity, prayed in many languages, with a group starting a decade in Spanish or English and the rest joining in our language of comfort. Mine was always Swahili.

Years later, when I meet people from that pilgrimage, we greet each other, saying, "I remember you from the walk!" We were truly a Church that goes forth. Far from our parish communities, we formed a new community on the road, and witnessed to our faith along the way.

> While relationships are more and more enacted on a global stage rather than localized in the context of a tight-knit community (for instance, the ability to connect virtually and so very easily with people in all corners of the globe), the requirement to make Jesus known, loved, and served has only become more indispensable. (page 92)

Pastor

Father Patrick A. Smith

While preparing to address the parents of religious-education students, I was struck by a profound thought: teaching the faith is like teaching a sport or a musical instrument; you learn by practicing! Only through practicing did I learn as a child how to swim, play basketball, or even sing on key. Only by doing each of these things through daily practice could I achieve what I loved and aspired. I learned how to become a Christian the same way. We all do.

In my home as a child, I learned to practice being a disciple of Jesus. When my parents and my Catholic school and parish offered opportunities for me to put my faith into practice, I learned how to respond to the Gospel I was being taught. Helping with the food drive at school or the toy drive at church, raking leaves, cutting grass, and shoveling snow for the elderly widow next door and across the street turned me from a religion student to a missionary disciple. If these opportunities to turn the Creed into deeds had not been made available to me, I would have learned about my Catholic faith but not how to respond to the Gospel of Christ. Neither would I have learned how to respond to Christ's invitation to enter a dynamic relationship with him. More than anything else, the encouragement to live my baptism and to put it into action made it possible for me to embrace my vocation to the priesthood. Teaching and catechizing without the chance to practice will render the baptized unresponsive to the call to evangelize. Just as science classes form scientists through laboratory work, parishes form disciples through local acts of discipleship during which children learn to respond to God's initiative.

Just as science classes form scientists through laboratory work, parishes form disciples through local acts of discipleship during which children learn to respond to God's initiative.

❖ Discussion Questions ❖

1. What can the parish do to connect people with formation opportunities on the parish and diocesan levels?

2. Are there formation programs that the parish could begin as a way of nurturing young people in ministry?

3. How can your parish show support for the oppressed in your community?

4. What opportunities does the parish offer for people to practice their faith in the community through corporal works of mercy?

5. Does the parish actively help people discern their gifts so that they can use them to respond to the Gospel?

Prayer

Hymn Suggestion

"Anthem," Tom Conry, GIA Publications, Inc., 1994.

Reading   (Mark 1:14–20)

After John had been arrested, Jesus came to Galilee proclaiming the gospel of God: "This is the time of fulfillment. The kingdom of God is at hand. Repent, and believe in the gospel."

As Jesus passed by the Sea of Galilee, he saw Simon and his brother Andrew casting their nets into the sea; they were fishermen. Jesus said to them, "Come after me, and I will make you fishers of men." Then they abandoned their nets and followed him. He walked along a little farther and saw James, the son of Zebedee, and his brother John. They too were in a boat mending their nets. Then he called them. So they left their father Zebedee in the boat along with the hired men and followed him.

Prayer of the Faithful

To our Lord, who calls us to be his witnesses, we pray:

❧ Reflection ❧

Jesus appears here like a magnet to Simon, Andrew, James, and John, who are drawn to him and abandoned their nets and their father, without question. This Gospel scene invites us to ponder our attraction to the Lord. When he calls us to respond to the work of the Gospel, perhaps in the silent presence of the poor or the sick among us, do we drop what we are doing at once and follow, or do we ask questions first and place limitations on our service? Do we give ourselves without reservation, or do we restrict our participation in the mission to which Christ invites us? Baptism demands that we preach the Gospel each day. Our vocation allows for no vacation.

✳ For vocations to the priesthood and religious life, and that all baptized Christians may serve the kingdom in love, we pray: **Lord, hear our prayer.**

✳ For the safety of those who serve their country in the military, we pray: **Lord, hear our prayer.**

✳ For those who reject the calling they have received, that the Lord may continue to draw them into service, we pray: **Lord, hear our prayer.**

✳ For the flourishing of the family, the domestic church, that the bonds of love within the household may grow ever stronger, we pray: **Lord, hear our prayer.**

✳ For those who will pass this day with nothing to eat and no one to care for their needs, we pray: **Lord, hear our prayer.**

✳ For all those for whom we have promised to pray, and for those who have no one to pray for them, we pray: **Lord, hear our prayer.**

Gathering our petitions, let us pray as the Lord taught us:

Our Father . . .

Collect

Merciful God,
listen to the faithful prayer of your Church.
Open our ears so that we may hear
the summons of our Lord Jesus.
Enflame our hearts with your Spirit
so that we may follow Christ with joy.
Help us to be disciples true.
Through our Lord Jesus Christ, your Son,
who lives and reigns with you in the unity of the Holy Spirit,
God, for ever and ever.
Amen.

CHAPTER 9

Built Up Together in the Spirit

[You are] built upon the foundation of the apostles and prophets,
with Christ Jesus himself as the capstone. Through him the whole
structure is held together and grows into a temple sacred in the
Lord; in him you also are being built together into a dwelling
place of God in the Spirit.

—Ephesians 2:20–22

In the early Church, as well as in the contemporary *Rite of Christian
Initiation of Adults*, the sacramental washing in the water of baptism
is followed immediately by the anointing with chrism (confirmation)
and then the gathering around the Lord's table to break the bread and
share the cup (Eucharist). Thus, the ancient pattern of initiation: baptism, confirmation, Eucharist are celebrated in one ritual event. There is
a structural unity to the sacraments of initiation when they are celebrated as part of one rite, with confirmation sealing baptism and
Eucharist linked closely to baptism.

Many Catholics are unaware of this ancient order of initiation,
instead believing that the way initiation is experienced today—with
baptism taking place in early infancy, Communion celebrated for the
first time at the age of reason (or age seven), and confirmation complet-
ing the initiation process in adolescence—is the way in which things
have always been done. Thus, they come to image the sacraments of
initiation as stepping-stones to be received as one matures along the

Christian way. When the sacraments are spread over this elongated period, we begin to conceive of them as achievement awards bestowed to mark progress. However, the sacraments of initiation, indeed all the sacraments of the Church, are neither about us nor about what we have accomplished. Instead, they are about Christ and what he is accomplishing in us for the salvation of the world.

Another way of stating this is that all sacraments concern our relationship with Christ. This relationship begins in the sacrament of baptism and unfolds throughout our Christian discipleship. The sacraments are about the way in which Christ is encountering us in order to use us to minister to others. Take for a moment the sacrament of reconciliation. Like the other sacraments, we have done damage to this sacrament by privatizing it and making it all about the individual penitent, when it is about the experience of mercy for the entire Church. This sacrament is far from a private celebration of God's love. Christ encounters the penitent in the celebration of the sacrament like the Father welcomes the prodigal son; the fatted calf is slaughtered so that the community can be called together to celebrate.[1] Our individual experience of forgiveness is meant to ignite the hearts of others to see and believe in God's gift of mercy. In other words, reconciliation is meant to ripple out into all parts of the world due to each individual encounter with Christ's gift of healing.

> The sacraments are about the way in which Christ is encountering us in order to use us to minister to others.

In addition to Catholics often interpreting the sacraments of initiation as achievement awards, confirmation, usually celebrated in the teen years, is often interpreted as the completion[2] of initiation, and thus

---

1. See Luke 15:11–32.

2. The *Catechism of the Catholic Church* (CCC) refers to confirmation as "completion." However, CCC, 1304, is clear that confirmation completes baptism. Indeed, it is the sacrament that seals baptism. Therefore, it is the sacrament that points toward the celebration of the Eucharist.

a sort of graduation from the faith. Young people interpret confirmation as the moment when they can choose for themselves whether they want to embrace the faith that was chosen for them by their parents at their baptism. However, in the celebration of the Eucharist, we profess our faith. Our reception of Communion is our *yes* to continue on the path of following after Christ. Thus, while the sacrament of confirmation is indeed a "completion" or a sealing of our baptism, it is the Eucharist that completes initiation. And because the Eucharist is celebrated again and again until paradise is entered, initiation into Christ is never completed. The journey of faith is continual: more and more is learned about the One whom we follow. Apprenticeship into Christ is a never-ending journey.

When confirmation is seen clearly as the sacrament that seals baptism and paves the way to the celebration of the Eucharist, not only will the need to reunite and reorder these initiation sacraments be understood, but there will be a better appreciation of the working of the Holy Spirit throughout the entirety of Christian life. It will be realized that we need the Holy Spirit to pour gifts upon us each day. Furthermore, through the work of discernment with other disciples, we will come to the realization that the gifts of the Spirit are not necessarily static—that is, we stand to be given new and amazing gifts at every turn in the road. Let us consider for a moment the working of the Holy Spirit in the baptism of the Lord as told by the evangelist Mark:

> It happened in those days that Jesus came from Nazareth in Galilee and was baptized in the Jordan by John. On coming out of the water he saw the heavens being torn open and the Spirit, like a dove, descending upon him. And a voice came from the heavens, "You are my beloved Son; with you I am well pleased." At once the Spirit drove him out into the desert, and he remained in the desert for forty days, tempted by Satan. He was among wild beasts, and angels ministered to him.[3]

---

3. Mark 1:9–13.

The earliest testimony of Jesus' baptism suggests that the Spirit serves two basic functions in relationship to the Lord. First, the Spirit provides some visible sign that accompanies the Father's voice in announcing the presence of his Son. Just as in the story of Noah sending the dove forth from the ark to testify to the dried earth (Genesis 8:6–12), so too does this dove associated with the regeneration of creation function at the Lord's baptism; in Jesus the covenant is restored, and the world begins anew. The second role of the Spirit in the account of the baptism is to send Jesus into mission, which begins with a time of formation in the desert. Thus, the Spirit both participates in making known the presence of the messiah and in the guidance of his mission.

The Holy Spirit continues to operate in the Church in exactly the same way. The Spirit has the dual role of heralding Christ and directing him (through the ministry of the Church) into mission. Think about the celebration of the Mass. The prayer that precedes the institution narrative, known as the *epiclesis*, calls for the descent of the Spirit upon the gifts of bread and wine, so that Christ may be present to the Church in our celebrating of the sacrament. According to Lukas Vischer, the epiclesis is "an expression of the impatient waiting for the coming of the kingdom. . . . It is a *maranatha*, a prayer that the Spirit will complete his work and bring everything under Christ."[4] Thus, the liturgical assembly requests the Father to make the risen Lord present to the community in a tangible way. It is by faith, that we believe the Spirit acts on our behalf. The Spirit, however, does not simply open our eyes to the presence of Christ; the Spirit unites us in Christ so that we might be sent in mission. This is the Spirit's second function. The faithful consume the Body and Blood of the Lord to grow deeper into his identity and to be commissioned anew to be sent forth into the world as "one body, one Spirit in Christ."[5] These two functions of the Holy Spirit serve to unite

---

4. Lukas Vischer, "The Epiclesis: Sign of Unity and Renewal," *Studia Liturgica* 6 (1969): 36.
5. See Eucharist Prayer III.

our daily work of discipleship with our participation in Christ's identity that is established at baptism. The working of the Spirit helps remind us that our labor in sowing together the world in mercy is really the work of the Lord. Our labor for the kingdom is inseparable from our common identity in Christ. Thus, the gifts of the Spirit that we celebrate in the sacrament of confirmation are not bestowed as personal property but rather as grace for mission.

The prayer that accompanies the laying on of hands at the celebration of confirmation within the context of the Easter Vigil reads as follows:

> Almighty God, Father of our Lord Jesus Christ,
> who brought these your servants to new birth
> by water and the Holy Spirit,
> freeing them from sin:
> send upon them, O Lord, the Holy Spirit, the Paraclete;
> give them the spirit of wisdom and understanding,
> the spirit of counsel and fortitude,
> the spirit of knowledge and piety
> fill them with the spirit of the fear of the Lord.[6]

This prayer makes the dual role of the Spirit abundantly clear: First comes our identity in Christ "by water and the Holy Spirit," then follows our being sent in mission by "the Paraclete." Daily discipleship calls for the daily discernment of gifts. Baptism invites us to explore together how the Holy Spirit is driving us out to embark on a new and exciting adventure in our journey of discipleship.

---

6. RCIA, 234.

❧ Pastoral Reflections ❧

Religious Educator

Cristina Castillo

Those of us fortunate to be witnesses during the first Communion and confirmation seasons know how special each sacrament and its celebrations are for the parish community. Unfortunately, many see the initiation sacraments as a list they must check off. During sacramental registrations, religious education staff and volunteers interact with families who are coming back to meet a requirement. During these times, we can show and explain in a few words what it means to be baptized, confirmed, and receive first Communion. At baptismal classes, parents should receive solid formation in their faith, which may lead to families who are more engaged and active in the parish. Formation for parents before their children's first Communion may encourage a deeper faith and connection to the parish.

No one journeys in their faith alone; companions assist us in navigating this path. When all participate and become involved, the community thrives. A few summers ago, I met Evelin while she was registering her children for the Rite of Christian Initiation of Adults. As I explained the process, it was easy to see that a feeling of shame came over Evelin as she mentioned that she had only been baptized. After her mother had left the Catholic faith, Evelin had been unable to receive her first Communion and confirmation. I encouraged her to become part of the Christian initiation process and to build on the formation she had received from her grandmother.

Throughout the process, Evelin was inquisitive, but most importantly, she was falling in love with her faith. Evelin, her children, and all those participating in the process were beginning to recognize God's presence in their lives through their parish community. Each of them witnessed how invested the community was in their formation and eagerly awaited the day they would receive their sacraments. Receiving the sacraments would be a deepening of their relationship with Christ and with each other. The sacraments bestow upon us the gifts necessary to move forward with our mission from God. Now, Evelin has embraced her mission to evangelize others by continuing her formation and becoming a catechist.

Music Minister

Michael Conrady

The high point of my year is assisting at the Easter Vigil. It is here that the ancient stories of salvation history are recounted. It is here that the news of Christ's resurrection is proclaimed. And it is here that the three sacraments of initiation are celebrated as the elect are baptized, confirmed, and receive the Eucharist.

Although most Catholics experience the initiation sacraments as three distinct events, the ancient ordering and connection of these sacraments comes into focus at the Great Vigil. At this liturgy, the community journeys with the elect on the holiest of nights, and the connection of the sacraments is apparent as the elect go from the water of the font to the anointing with sacred chrism, to the Lord's table.

Like many of the people who attend the Easter Vigil, I journey with the catechumens and candidates during the Christian initiation process throughout the year. This journeying occurs both in the public life of the community during the celebration of the rites and during sessions in which I speak on music and liturgy.

> So it is that on this night, we welcome our new brothers and sisters in the Lord at the table for the first time as we experience the mystery of discipleship—dying to be reborn, united in one Lord, one faith, and one baptism.

As a Church gathered on the night of the Vigil, we are invested in the lives of those who stand before the font. In journeying with these men and women, we recall our baptism, our anointing at confirmation, and our first Eucharist. From the waters of rebirth, through the sealing of the Holy Spirit, to uniting our lives with Christ's sacrifice on the altar, we say yes to God's call. We call on the Holy Spirit to unite us so that we too may be broken and sent out into the world. So it is that on this night, we welcome our new brothers and sisters in the Lord at the table for the first time as we experience the mystery of discipleship—dying to be reborn, united in one Lord, one faith, and one baptism.

Volunteer Coordinator Caroline Okello

A few summers ago, I coordinated a trip for six parishioners to be part of a week-long immersion experience in El Paso, Texas, and Juárez, Mexico. The aim of this experience, organized by Maryknoll Brothers and Fathers, was to expose participants to the realities at the US-Mexican border, where thousands were gathering as they escaped violence and poverty in their countries. During this week, participants listened to immigrants and those who worked with them, members from the border patrol, and an immigration attorney. The issues at the border are complex and can be divisive, but this immersion trip gave participants an opportunity to see, learn, judge, and analyze for themselves in light of the Gospel.

During the trip, I shared photos of our daily activities and events on our parish Facebook page, so that community members and friends could join us virtually. Even though this was an immersion trip with a focus on learning, some of our group were natural doers and cleaned the dormitories, arranged clothing, and packed bags for those departing for the United States.

On our return, parishioners packed a room to hear participants, one by one, share their experience, telling how they had been touched. Tearfully, some of them tried to express the helplessness they felt in the face of so much suffering. One participant said, "I came away saddened, disappointed, but also incredibly inspired. So often we focus on how terrible things are. But I saw so many selfless people working at the border. It was fascinating, complex, confusing, ever-changing, disappointing, and inspiring."

The presence of the Holy Spirit is not always recognized. But when sadness and disappointment drive action to create positive changes, we can be sure that the Spirit is with us. As Stephen S. Wilbricht states, "The Spirit unites us in Christ so that we might be sent in mission" (page 106).

> The presence of the Holy Spirit is not always recognized. But when sadness and disappointment drive action to create positive changes, we can be sure that the Spirit is with us.

Pastor

Father Patrick A. Smith

For good reason, I experienced an acute sense of inadequacy and unworthiness prior to ordination: I was both. But glancing over the Scriptures, I noticed that, over and over, the people God called had a similar reaction. Abraham told God that he and Sarah were too old to have a son (Genesis 17:17). Moses informed God that he didn't speak well enough to confront the pharaoh (Exodus 4:10). Jeremiah said he was too young to be a prophet

(Jeremiah 1:6). These ancestors of our faith felt inadequate and unworthy of the call because without God's help they were.

I have come to understand that the Christian life is about our availability to the Spirit and not our abilities. How do we make ourselves available? For me, it's daily prayer. Prayer is to the disciple what a charger is to the cellphone. With no charger, there is no power to do or achieve what you have been created to accomplish. For this reason, in every parish I have been assigned, I have sought to help my parishioners establish a daily habit of prayer. Through prayer, they connect with the source of their spiritual strength.

Prayer opens us to allow God to live within us. People who understand that the Christian life is about *inhabitation* before it is about *imitation* (for example, of Jesus) are less likely to exhaust themselves trying to act like Jesus and follow his teaching without relying on the only One who can make that possible: the Holy Spirit. The *Catechism of the Catholic Church*, 1213, states: "Holy Baptism is the basis of the whole Christian life, the gateway to life in the Spirit." Having entered through the gate, it is time to step into the life, empowered by the Holy Spirit to go and bear fruit that will last.

❖ Discussion Questions ❖

1. How have you seen relationships in your parish further the building up of the Church?

2. What can the parish do to connect parishioners so that efforts will be joined in the building up together of the community?

3. Our baptismal calling is to go forth past the boundaries of the parish. How can the parish work together to build up the larger community?

4. Prayer needs to be at the foundation of all that we do. How does the parish lead people to root their lives in prayer?

5. Does the parish help people explore how the Holy Spirit is driving them to embark on a new adventure in discipleship?

Prayer

Hymn Suggestion

"Glorious in Majesty," Jeff Cothran, GIA Publications, Inc., 1972.

Reading John 16:12–15

[Jesus said to his disciples:] "I have much more to tell you, but you cannot bear it now. But when he comes, the Spirit of truth, he will guide you to all truth. He will not speak on his own, but he will speak what he hears, and will declare to you the things that are coming. He will glorify me, because he will take from what is mine and declare it to you. Everything that the Father has is mine; for this reason I told you that he will take from what is mine and declare it to you."

> ### ❧ Reflection ❧
>
> One of the characteristics of divinity that Jesus reveals is that God is mutual sharing, or what in theological language is called *perichoresis*. Whatever belongs to the Father belongs to the Son and the Spirit, and vice versa. No person of the Holy Trinity claims sole ownership of anything; all is shared in love. As Jesus tells his disciples, the Spirit "will take from what is mine and declare it to you." We are the recipients of grace. How responsible are we with all that God has given us through Christ in the Holy Spirit? How willing are we to pour forth upon others the grace that has been so lavishly bestowed upon us?

Prayer of the Faithful

To the Lord, who builds us up into one body in the Spirit, we pray:

✳ That all baptized into Christ may seek to deepen their knowledge of love of the Triune God, we pray:
Hear us, O Lord.

＊ That all members of the Body of Christ may share their resources fully with the less fortunate and may provide an image of divine unity for the world to follow, we pray:
Hear us, O Lord.

＊ That all parents may teach their children from a very young age the importance of sharing and not hoarding, we pray:
Hear us, O Lord.

＊ That we may all participate in leading our parish community by freely declaring unto others the grace we have been given, we pray:
Hear us, O Lord.

＊ That all those who have died may be welcomed into the halls of heaven with the entire communion of saints, we pray:
Hear us, O Lord.

Gathering our petitions, let us pray as the Lord taught us:

Our Father . . .

Collect

Triune God,
you reveal yourself to us
as a perfect relationship of love:
three Persons, one God.
From the teaching of your Son,
we learn that what is poured upon us
is meant to be shared with others.
Send your Spirit upon your Church,
and help us to grow in charity and love.
Through Christ our Lord.
Amen.

CHAPTER 10

Baptism as the Bond of Unity

Baptism, therefore, establishes a sacramental bond of unity among all who through it are reborn.

—Decree on Ecumenism, 22

The fundamental statement from the *Decree on Ecumenism, Unitatis redintegratio* (UR), on baptism establishing a sacramental bond of unity among all who are reborn through it is immediately followed by the sentence: "But baptism, of itself, is only a beginning, a point of departure, for it is wholly directed toward the acquiring of fullness of life in Christ."[1] The point is simple: Baptism requires daily effort. Christians are made, not born, and they are called upon to continually grow until perfect union is realized in the final kingdom.

When the bishops gathered during the first half of the 1960s (from 1962 through 1965) to consider ecumenism, among all the many topics to be raised during the Second Vatican Council, it was quite common to hear the traditional teaching touted that "outside the Church, there is no salvation" (*extra ecclesiam nulla salus*). Associated with the writings of Cyprian of Carthage in the third century,[2] this term came to be applied not only to non-Christians but to Christians who separated from the

---

1. UR, 22.

2. See Ormond Rush, *The Vision of Vatican II: Its Fundamental Principles* (Collegeville, MN: Liturgical Press, 2019), 372.

Catholic Church as a result of the Protestant Reformation. This teaching became increasingly problematic, especially as the Church continued to encounter people of other cultures through the spread of colonialism. Pope Pius XII, in his encyclical *Mystici corporis*, written in 1943, attempted to broaden the parameters of salvation when he wrote: "[B]y an unconscious desire and longing, they (non-Catholics) have a certain relationship with the Mystical Body of the Redeemer."[3]

Several years prior to *Mystici corporis*, the Dominican ecclesiologist Yves Congar wrote that true ecumenism means believing that a non-Catholic Christian is a Christian not *despite* his separated community of faith but because of it. Congar contends:

> Ecumenism begins when it is admitted that others, not only individuals but ecclesiastical bodies as well, may also be right though they differ from us; that they too have truth, holiness and gifts of God even though they do not profess our form of Christianity. There is ecumenism, says an active member of this movement, when it is believed that others are Christian not in spite of their particular confession but in it and by it. Such a conviction governs that complex of ideas which make up the ecumenical attitude—respect for other confessions and the action of the Holy Spirit in them, the sense and the avowal of the past sins, limitation and failures of one's own confession, the desire to know about the other confessions and the gifts of God to them and to enter into friendly relations with them, and, pending full unity, as far as possible into effective communion.[4]

Congar's description of true ecumenism demands a shift in attitude that quite possibly still needs to be made by many Catholics today. While it is true that the radical separation that constituted relationships between Catholics and Protestants in the middle of the twentieth century has

---

3. Pius XII, *Mystici corporis*, 103.

4. Yves Congar, *Divided Christendom: A Catholic Study of the Problem of Reunion* (London: Geoffrey Bles, 1939), 135–136. Quote taken from Rush, *The Vision of Vatican II*, 373–374.

softened tremendously—witnessed simply in the ease of families condoning and celebrating interdenominational marriages today—does there not remain a lingering air of superiority on the part of Catholics? In other words, is it not the case that ecumenism for most Catholics means luring other Christians into the Catholic fold?

Congar's challenge is clear: real ecumenism comes down to believing that the Holy Spirit gifts other Christians just as much as Catholic Christians, "when it is believed that others are Christian not in spite of their particular confession but in it and by it." Congar suggests that the "ecumenical attitude" consists of the following:

One cannot truly learn and understand other Christian communities if he or she approaches this study by holding on to the belief that Catholicism holds the only truth. Ecumenism requires genuine openness and humility.

* respect for the working of the Holy Spirit in other Christian communities;

* admission of the past sins and failures in one's own church;

* learning about other ways of approaching the Christian faith;

* establishing friendly relations based on dialogue and prayer.

Ecumenism is an investment that takes work and sacrifice. One cannot truly learn and understand other Christian communities if he or she approaches this study by holding on to the belief that Catholicism holds the only truth. Ecumenism requires genuine openness and humility.

The *Decree on Ecumenism* is clear in the way in which effort should be taken to join hands with all Christians and learn from them our differences and our similarities. Furthermore, it suggests that there is much that diverse Christians can do together to carry out the work of building up the world in unity:

> The Christian way of life of these our sisters and brothers is nourished by faith in Christ. It is strengthened by the grace of baptism

and by hearing the word of God. This way of life expresses itself in private prayer, in meditation on the scriptures, in the life of a Christian family, and in the worship of the community gathered together to praise God. Furthermore, their worship sometimes displays notable features of a liturgy once shared in common. The faith by which they believe in Christ bears fruit in praise and thanksgiving for the benefits received from the hands of God. Joined to it is a lively sense of justice and a true charity toward others. This active faith has been responsible for many organizations for the relief of spiritual and material distress, the advancement of the education of youth, the improvement of social conditions of life, and the promotion of peace throughout the world.[5]

Notice that this paragraph never mentions the word *doctrine*. It suggests instead that commonality, or a sense of unity in diversity, may be discovered in discerning the Christian life (that is, the ways in which Christians might unite to educate, to heal, to pray, and to promote justice and peace throughout the world). In fact, Pope Francis can be said to lead by emphasizing the way in which Christians live rather than examining the teachings they believe. In the midst of the Year of Mercy, Francis stated:

"[T]he true defenders of doctrine are not those who uphold its letter, but its spirit; not ideas but people; not formulae but the gratuitousness of God's love and forgiveness. . . . The Church's first duty is not to hand down condemnations or anathemas, but to proclaim God's mercy, to call to conversion, and to lead all men and women to salvation in the Lord."[6]

---

5. UR, 23.

6. Pope Francis, "Address at the Conclusion of the Synod of Bishops" (October 24, 2015). http://www.vatican.va/content/francesco/en/speeches/2015/october/documents/papa -francesco_20151024_sinodo-conclusione-lavori.html. Quote found in Gaillardetz, "Ecclesial Belonging in This Time of Scandal," 201–202.

Following Congar's agenda of respect, contrition, education, and friendship, there is so much that Christians can do together to show the desire to develop the unity begun in our common baptism. Ponder these questions for a moment: When was the last time you heard a homily that addressed the need to work on respect and friendship with Christians outside the Catholic Church? Are we taking seriously the need to become educated about the history and traditions of other Christian communities? If not, how can we truly come to respect the differences that make them gifted by the Spirit? Therefore, leaders must make the agenda of ecumenism apparent in the parish. Our members need to be challenged to stretch out their hands in friendship and to collaborate in works of charity and love. We need to come together in prayer and to celebrate what makes us different as well as to celebrate what makes us one.

❧ Pastoral Reflections ❧

Religious Educator   Cristina Castillo

A few years ago, when our community experienced a damaging rainstorm, the parish was left without a physical church for worship services. The neighboring Christian community opened its doors and lent its hall to our Catholic community. With homes damaged of both parishioners and the members of the neighboring Christian community, people of both communities collected toiletries and clothes and arranged shelter locations for anyone who was displaced.

In baptism, we are united to the local and universal Church. We are also connected to everyone else in the world, Catholic and non-Catholic, aside from having responsibilities toward the rest of humanity and creation. At times we seem to forget about our brothers and sisters who might belong to other religions. In many areas of the country, dialogue with non-Catholics is rare. Over and over, Pope Francis asks us to go out into the world, to be a Church that engages with everyone in the world. We are asked to become active shepherds. Shepherds who, like Jesus, did not care if he was speaking to a leper or a Samaritan.

Like Jesus, we too have an influential role in the lives of many. We have gifts bestowed upon us by the Holy Spirit, and we should use them to promote the common good. In the area of religious education, we can introduce collaborative work with other Christians. Opportunities can be created for our communities to come together and interact. After all, we are all striving for a better world. The strength in our faith would be the light leading the work. In many cases, these communities are already collaborating.

Coming together as one can take many shapes or forms. We can come together in times of need, and we can also gather to dialogue about how we can continue helping and guiding people to God. We can also come together to continue working for the common good and love of neighbor. Above all, we need to be proactive and genuine in these relationships, making sure we can help one another and focus on the Holy Spirit as we collaborate.

> Coming together as one can take many shapes or forms. . . . Above all, we need to be proactive and genuine in these relationships, making sure we can help one another and focus on the Holy Spirit as we collaborate.

Music Minister

Michael Conrady

Could you imagine attending a Catholic church at which a Methodist pastor delivered the homily? What about an evangelical preacher? Besides being a violation of canon law, it would probably seem out of the ordinary. And yet you might not think twice about singing Charles Wesley's "Hark! the Herald Angels Sing" at Mass, or the popular "Seek Ye First," which is a product of the American evangelical church.

In almost any Catholic hymnal today are hymns sourced from a wide variety of denominations, countries, and centuries. (Even Gregorian chant borrowed an occasional text or melody.) These songs are very much products of their respective contexts, but they are appropriate for Catholic worship because their truths transcend denominational barriers.

As Catholics, we are called to engage in ecumenism. We recognize our common baptism with members of other denominations. To be sure, there may be doctrinal differences among baptized Christians, but we are not threatened by the presence of the Holy Spirit in other communities. Respectful dialogue is essential as we work toward unity.

At my parish, people from other faith traditions often join our choir. There are various reasons they may be prompted to join our music ministry, but it is not from any lack of oversight on our part. Membership in our choir is open to any baptized person. Sometimes the Holy Spirit eventually prompts them to join the Catholic Church but not always. The parish respects their gifts, their calling, and the work of the Holy Spirit in their lives.

In my more than twenty-five years of leading Catholic music programs, I have been honored to participate in many ecumenical musical events where the inspiration and truths shared via music made great strides in uniting Christians in prayer and purpose. I cannot help but believe that this making and sharing of music is pleasing to the Lord. Sometimes I think that it is no coincidence that pastoral musicians are often the ones leading the way in the efforts towards ecumenism.

Volunteer Coordinator   Caroline Okello

The bond of unity of which I write is a bond that I felt with so many people as I sought to see Pope Francis when he came to the United States. And not only that, as a member of the Serra Club, I planned to witness the canonization of Junipero Serra, the Franciscan priest who helped bring the faith to California. The problem in my plan was that I did not have a ticket to the canonization ceremony. Prior to departing for the event in Washington, DC, I had asked everyone I could think of, for a ticket to the ceremony, to no avail. All the way I prayed to God to allow me to attend the canonization.

While checking into the hotel where Serrans would stay, a woman in line heard me say that my roommate had backed out. She was in a similar predicament and asked if we could share a room. I jumped at that offer to save money. At the all-Serra meeting that night, and then as I readied for bed, I continued to pray for a ticket.

My roommate, whose son is a bishop, told me that there seemed to be no chance of my attending the canonization. But she encouraged me to see the pope after his visit to the White House the next morning. Painfully, I accepted my fate, and by 4:00 AM the next day, dressed in my cultural regalia, I lined up by the White House with thousands of people waiting to see the pope, whose meeting with President Barack Obama was to end at 11:00 AM.

Just before Pope Francis, in the popemobile, passed where I stood, I received a voicemail message from my roommate. "Caroline, I have a ticket for you to attend the canonization. The bus departs the hotel at 1:00 PM if you can make it." I jumped with joy, but my joy was cut short when reality hit. I was in the middle of a multitude of people and even after the pope was gone, it would take a while to get out. Determined, I started forward. When the gates opened, I was among the first out. Dressed as I was, running was not easy, but I made it to a cab and pleaded with the driver to get me to the hotel quickly. I arrived in time to jump in the bus.

Looking at the ticket, I asked my roommate, "Are you the angel God used to deliver my ticket?" Later, my friend who stayed behind expressed admiration for my faith. I cannot take the credit and am glad the Holy Spirit inspired me to forge on, and God worked with my little faith. Jesus said, "Because of your little faith. Amen, I say to you, if you have faith the size of a mustard seed, you will say to this mountain, 'Move from here to there,' and it will move. Nothing will be impossible for you" (Matthew 17:20).

Pastor

Father Patrick A. Smith

As a Black Catholic priest who has spent nearly all my ordained ministry in predominantly Black Catholic parishes, racism has proven to be the greatest obstacle to my work of evangelization in our community. More than any other scandal in the Church in the United States, racial injustice has undermined the efforts of the Church to win over the souls of Black Americans for Christ and bring them into the sheepfold of the Catholic community.

Among other things, racism is the antithesis of the unity for which Christ prayed: "I pray not only for them, but also for those who will believe in me through their word, so that they may all be one, as you, Father are in me and I in you, that they also may be in us, that the world may believe that you sent me" (John 17:20–21). Jesus' prayer states the most compelling reason for pursuing unity: that the world may come to believe in him as the One whom God sent to save us!

To the degree that ordained bishops and baptized laity are unwilling to address the scandal of racism in the Church, the more the lie endures that Black people are neither equal nor welcome in Christ's Church. Yet I still have hope and faith in the One who prayed for the unity of his bride, the Church. My parents, aunts, and uncles did, too. My parents had all their children baptized and raised them Catholics. Though denied a Catholic school education themselves due to segregation, my parents pooled their funds to see that all their children received at least twelve years of Catholic schooling. My uncle, once physically escorted out of Mass for sitting in the "whites only" pews at the front of the church, enjoyed seeing me preside as pastor of the same church decades later. Despite racism, my elders persevered in witnessing to the unity of Christ among all the baptized by never confusing the message with the messengers. My Catholic foundation can be attributed to their courageous faith in Christ. In return, my perseverance in the faith today serves as a tribute to them.

Though denied a Catholic school education themselves due to segregation, my parents pooled their funds to see that all their children received at least twelve years of Catholic schooling.

❖ Discussion Questions ❖

1. Is your parish connected to other Christian communities? If not, what can be done to join the parish with an ecclesial community? Is there a community that needs your parish's support?

2. Are there people from other denominations who participate in ministries or activities at your parish? How are they welcomed?

3. What does the parish do to support people in their daily efforts to live out their baptism and be attentive to the work of the Holy Spirit in their lives?

4. How can your parishioners work toward a unity in the Church with people of all races?

5. How can the parish help people to regard their baptism with humility and realize that the Holy Spirit gifts non-Catholics as well as Catholics?

Prayer

Hymn Suggestion

"They'll Know We Are Christians," F.E.L. Publications, LTD, 1966.

Reading   Colossians 3:12–16

Put on then, as God's chosen ones, holy and beloved, heartfelt compassion, kindness, humility, gentleness, and patience, bearing with one another and forgiving one another, if one has a grievance against another; as the Lord has forgiven you, so must you also do. And over all these put on love, that is, the bond of perfection. And let the peace of Christ control your hearts, the peace into which you were also called in one body. And be thankful. Let the word of Christ dwell in you richly, as in all wisdom you teach and admonish one another, singing psalms, hymns, and spiritual songs with gratitude in your hearts to God.

> ### ❧ Reflection ❧
>
> Paul's correspondence to the Colossians presents us with a list of priorities for living the Christian way of life. We are called by Christ to live as members of his one Body. Parts of the Body must work together for its full and healthy functioning. Does a rupture in the relationship of two Christians have an impact on the entire Body? Absolutely! Notice that it is not the responsibility of the Head alone to admonish or challenge members of the Body. Each of us has a role to play in maintaining the "body of perfection" which unites us. Division within the Body of Christ ought to be a scandal that calls for constant repair and renewal.

Prayer of the Faithful

To the Lord, who puts peace in our hearts, we pray:

✳ For our pope, all bishops, priests, and deacons, that they may help to knit us together as one Body in Christ, we pray: **Lord, have mercy.**

✳ For all members of Christ's Body, that our ecumenical gatherings and dialogue may witness to the love that unites us, we pray: **Lord, have mercy.**

✳ For a spirit of reconciliation to guide the way of all those at enmity with others, we pray: **Lord, have mercy.**

✳ For all those who feel severed from Christ's Body, especially the divorced and remarried, we pray: **Lord, have mercy.**

✳ For the dead, who continue to remain connected to the Body from their place before God's throne, we pray: **Lord, have mercy.**

Gathering our petitions, we pray as the Lord taught us:

Our Father . . .

Collect

Lord Jesus Christ,
you form in your Church your one Body
and command that we sacrifice
our individual pursuits for its good.
May we work to unite
all Christians in the bond of your love
and so call all the world to respond to the needs of the kingdom.
You live and reign with the Father
in the unity of the Holy Spirit,
God, for ever and ever.
Amen.

BIBLIOGRAPHY

❖

Baptism, Eucharist and Ministry. Faith and Order Paper, no. 111. Geneva: World Council of Churches, 1982.

The Book of Common Prayer and Administration of the Sacraments and Other Rites and Ceremonies of the Church . . . According to the Use of the Episcopal Church. New York: Seabury Press, 1979.

Cahalan, Kathleen A. "Toward a Fundamental Theology of Ministry." *Worship* 80 (2006): 102–120.

Catechism of the Catholic Church. Rome: Libreria Editrice Vaticana, 1994.

Codd, Kevin A. "'I Am a Pilgrim on the Earth': The Pilgrim Way." *Worship* 84 (2010): 154–170.

Code of Canon Law, Latin-English Edition. Washington, DC: Canon Law Society of America, 1983.

Cones, Bryan. "'How Beautiful the Feet': Discerning the Assembly's Path on Holy Thursday." In *Liturgy with a Difference: Beyond Inclusion in the Christian Assembly,* edited by Stephen Burns and Bryan Cones, 3–18. London: SMC Press, 2019.

Cones, Bryan, and Stephen Burns. "Introduction: The Vivid Richness of God's Image." In *Liturgy with a Difference: Beyond Inclusion in the Christian Assembly,* edited by Stephen Burns and Bryan Cones, xiii–xix. London: SMC Press, 2019.

Congar, Yves. *Divided Christendom: A Catholic Study of the Problem of Reunion.* London: Geoffrey Bless, 1939.

Doak, Mary. *A Prophetic Public Church: Witness to Hope amid the Global Crises of the Twenty-First Century.* Collegeville, MN: Liturgical Press, 2020.

Ehle, Mary. *Anointed for Discipleship: The Meaning of Baptism for Our Christian Life.* Chicago: Liturgy Training Publications, 2019, 2022.

Evans, Bernard. *Glorifying the Lord by Your Life: Catholic Social Teaching and the Liturgy.* Chicago: Liturgy Training Publications, 2020.

Fahey, Michael A. "Church." In *Systematic Theology: Roman Catholic Perspectives*, vol. 2., edited by Francis Schüssler Fiorenza and John Galvin, 4–74. Minneapolis, MN: Fortress Press, 1991.

Flannery, Austin, ed. *The Basic Sixteen Documents: Vatican Council II Constitutions, Decrees, Declarations.* Northport, NY: Costello Publishing Company, 1996.

Francis. "Address at the Conclusion of the Synod of Bishops" (October 24, 2015). http://www.vatican.va/content/francesco/en/speeches/2015/october/documents/papa-francesco_20151024_sinodo-conclusione-lavori.html.

_____. *Evangelii gaudium* (*The Joy of the Gospel*). Apostolic letter. November 24, 2013.

Gaillardetz, Richard R. "Ecclesial Belonging in This Time of Scandal." *Worship* 94 (2020): 196–204.

_____. "In Service of Communion: A Trinitarian Foundation of Christian Ministry." *Worship* 67 (1993): 418–431.

Gallup. "Catholics' Church Attendance Resumes Downward Slide" (April 9, 2018). https://news.gallup.com/poll/232226/church-attendance-among-catholics-resumes-downward-slide.aspx.

John Paul II. *Pastores dabo vobis* (*I Shall Give You Shepherds*). Apostolic letter. March 15, 1992.

_____. *Redemptoris missio* (*The Mission of the Redeemer*). Encyclical letter. December 7, 1990.

_____. *Sollicitudo rei socialis* (*The Social Concern*). Encyclical letter. December 30, 1987.

Joslyn-Siemiatkoski, Daniel E., and Ruth A. Meyers. "The Baptismal Ecclesiology of *Holy Women, Holy Men*: Developments in the Theology of Sainthood in the Episcopal Church." *Anglican Theological Review* 94 (2012): 27–36.

Kasper, Walter. "Ecclesiological and Ecumenical Implications of Baptism." *The Ecumenical Review* 52 (2000): 526–541.

Lawler, Michael G., and Thomas Shanahan. "The Church Is a Graced Communion." *Worship* 67 (1993): 484–501.

McGann, Mary E. *The Meal That Reconnects: Eucharistic Eating and the Global Food Crisis*. Collegeville, MN: Liturgical Press, 2020.

Michel, Virgil. "Natural and Supernatural Society." *Orate Fratres* 10 (1936): 243–247, 293–296, 338–342, 394–398, 434–438.

Myers, C. Kilmer. *Baptized into the One Church*. New York: Seabury Press, 1963.

Order of Baptism of Children. Chicago: Liturgy Training Publications, 2020.

Orsy, Ladislas. *Discernment: Theology and Practice, Communal and Personal*. Collegeville, MN: Liturgical Press, 2020.

Paul VI. *Evangelii nuntiandi* (*Evangelization in the World*). Encyclical letter. December 8, 1975.

Philibert, Paul J. "Reclaiming the Vision of an Apostolic Church." *Worship* 83 (2009): 482–501.

Pius XII. *Mystici corporis* (*The Mystical Body of Christ*). Encyclical letter. June 29, 1943.

Provodedo, Elizabeth. "Pope Formalizes Women's Roles but Priesthood Stays Out of Reach." *The New York Times* (January 11, 2021). https://www.nytimes.com/2021/01/11/world/europe/pope-women .html.

Rite of Christian Initiation of Adults, Study Edition. Chicago: Liturgy Training Publications, 1988.

Rush, Ormond. *The Vision of Vatican II: Its Fundamental Principles.* Collegeville, MN: Liturgical Press, 2019.

Searle, Mark. "The Act of Communion: A Commentary." *Assembly* 4 (1978): 4, 6–7.

————. "Grant Us Peace. . . . Do We Hear What We Are Saying?" In *Rehearsing God's Just Kingdom: The Eucharistic Vision of Mark Searle*, by Stephen S. Wilbricht, 215–227. Collegeville, MN: Liturgical Press, 2013.

————. "Serving the Lord with Justice." In *Liturgy and Social Justice*, edited by Mark Searle, 13–35. Collegeville, MN: Liturgical Press, 1980.

Sullivan, Robert David. "Parishes without Pastors Decline, But Only Because More Churches Have Closed." *America* (June 14, 2019). https://www.americamagazine.org/faith/2019/06/14/parishes -without-pastors-decline-only-because-more-churches-have-closed.

United States Catholic Bishops. *Disciples Called to Witness: The New Evangelization*. Washington, DC: United States Conference of Catholic Bishops, 2012.

————. *Economic Justice for All: Pastoral Letter on Catholic Social Teaching and the U.S. Economy*. Washington, DC: National Conference of Catholic Bishops, 1986.

Van Gennep, Arnold. *The Rites of Passage*. Chicago: University of Chicago Press, 1969.

Vischer, Lukas. "The Epiclesis: Sign of Unity and Renewal." *Studia Liturgica* 6 (1969): 30–39.

Weil, Louis. "Baptismal Ecclesiology: Uncovering a Paradigm." In *Equipping the Saints: Ordination in Anglicanism Today,* edited by Ronald L. Dowling and David R. Holeton, 18–34. Dublin: Columba Press, 2006.

Wilbricht, Stephen S. *Baptismal Ecclesiology and the* Order of Christian Funerals. Chicago: Liturgy Training Publications, 2018.

Wood, Susan K. "Conclusion: Convergence Points toward a Theology of Ordered Ministries." In *Ordering the Baptismal Priesthood: Theologies of Lay and Ordained Ministry,* edited by Susan K. Wood, 256–267. Collegeville, MN: Liturgical Press, 2003.

Zimmerman, Mark. "Pope Wants Priests to be Shepherds Who Encounter Their Flocks." *Crux* (June 16, 2017). https://cruxnow.com/vatican /2017/06/pope-wants-priests-shepherds-encounter-flocks.

ABOUT THE AUTHOR

✤

Stephen S. Wilbricht, a religious of the Congregation of Holy Cross, is an associate professor in the Department of Religious Studies and Theology at Stonehill College in Easton, Massachusetts. Prior to pursuing a doctorate in liturgical studies at the Catholic University of America in Washington, DC, he enjoyed seven years of pastoral ministry in two parishes in the Phoenix area. He has been a member of the North American Academy of Liturgy since 2011, participating in the work of the Christian Initiation Seminar. His major research interests revolve around the work of the liturgical movement and issues of present-day liturgical renewal. He is the author of *Rehearsing God's Just Kingdom: The Eucharistic Vision of Mark Searle* (Liturgical Press, 2013), *The Role of the Priest in Christian Initiation* (Liturgy Training Publications, 2017), and *Baptismal Ecclesiology and the* Order of Christian Funerals (Liturgy Training Publications, 2018).

ABOUT THE ARTIST

✤

James B. Janknegt lives and paints in Elgin, Texas. He has exhibited his paintings widely throughout Texas and Washington, DC, and in the Museum of Biblical Art in New York. He has a bachelor of fine arts degree from the University of Texas at Austin and a master of arts degree and a master of fine arts degree from the University of Iowa in studio art. More of his work can be seen at www.bcartfarm.com.